Readers' experiences with the *B*

M000249025

*I had been doing daily meditative work w*
*for over a year, and loved the progress I made in coming to understand myself. With the Book of Days series, the depth of my understanding has increased almost faster than I could keep up. The clarity and positive tone of the writing resonates, and leaves me feeling reborn and in harmony with the universe every day.*

– **Paula Mooney**, nurse, gardener & herbalist (Bigelow, AR)

*Terah's presentation of the angels as 'angles' of light within us has enabled me to approach the concept of angels for the first time in my life. I have always been hesitant, if not suspect, of religious or spiritual concepts that put "God" unattainably outside of us. The intimacy and loving relevance of these daily wisdoms have truly awakened me to the 'Divine within' – and with the power of the daily practice my awareness just keeps growing.*

– **Stacie Florer**, jewelry artist, writer & teacher (Asheville, NC)

*A wonderful expansion on the original book, the dailies are a compass for me and a sanctuary to enfold my day. I take the current volume with me when I hike in the mountains. Can you imagine what it's like to read these messages high up among the trees, next to a mountain river or lake – sitting in a forest that is filled with the breath of God and all creation?*

**– Aletheia Mystea**, psychotherapist & founder of Green Theology Ministries: Earth Rites, Animal Rites, Human Rites (Fort Collins CO)

*I am totally thrilled that the Book of Days series was born of the original Birth Angels work. Building upon the immensely insightful text describing the Tree of Life and the angelic aspects, these new books go deeper into an ancient spiritual tradition that was previously unknown to me. I have found this work to be very meaningful, and have incorporated some of the teachings into my daily spiritual practice for inspiration, guidance and comfort.*

– **Judith Clements**, Educator (Tampa, FL)

*There have been so many times when the daily wisdom addressed something that was happening on that day, and so they focus me every day, bringing more awareness to my actions and thoughts. The concept of angels as "angles of light" made it easier to assimilate their wisdoms into my everyday life. Above all, the daily angels bring me back to myself by illuminating the parts of me that make up the "whole" of everything.*

– **Lindy Labriola**, student, writer & singer-songwriter (Amherst, MA)

*I love the depth of this follow-up to the first Birth Angels book – you get a powerful sense of the presence of the Angels through the wisdoms and even throughout the introductory material. I also appreciate the updates in this edition concerning the historical background.*

– **Jodi Lynn**, Actor (New York, NY)

TERAH COX

# BIRTH ANGELS

## *Book of Days*

### Daily Wisdoms with the 72 Angels of the Tree of Life

Volume 1: March 21 ~ June 2

**Terah Cox**

Blessings and warmest wishes Terah

Stone's Throw Publishing House
Second Edition, March 2015

**BIRTH ANGELS BOOK OF DAYS**
*Daily Wisdoms with the 72 Angels of the Tree of Life*
**Volume 1: March 21 ~ June 2**

Series includes:
**Volume 1: March 21 – June 2**
**Volume 2: June 3 – August 16**
**Volume 3: August 17 – October 29**
**Volume 4: October 30 – January 8**
**Volume 5: January 9 – March 20**

**Stone's Throw Publishing House**
ISBN-13: 978-0692405765
ISBN-10: 0692405763
Second Edition Softcover | Volume 1: March 2015
Second Kindle Digital Edition | Volume 1: March 2015

First Edition Softcover | Volume 1: April 2014
First Kindle Digital Edition | Volume 1: March 2014



For permissions, information about author and additional books and materials, see
www.terahcox.com
www.72BirthAngels.com

---

Book design by Terah Cox | Author photo by Gittel Price
Wing detail of Fresco Angel by Giotto di Bondone,
Scenes from the Life of Christ #4 (1304-06)

---

# Books by Terah Cox

---

**BIRTH ANGELS BOOK OF DAYS ~ Vols. 1 - 5**
**Daily Wisdoms with the 72 Angels of the Tree of Life**
Stone's Throw Publishing House (Vols. 1-5, 2014-2015)

**THE STORY OF LOVE & TRUTH**
Stone's Throw Publishing House
Limited Handmade Edition (2007)
Illustrated Softcover Edition (2011)

**BIRTH ANGELS ~ Fulfilling Your Life Purpose with the 72 Angels of the Kabbalah**
Andrews McMeel/Simon & Schuster (2004)
(acquired by Stone's Throw Publishing House 2013)
Greek edition: Asimakis Publishing, Athens, Greece (2014)
Czech edition: Barevny Svet s.r.o (2016)

**YOU CAN WRITE SONG LYRICS**
Writers Digest / F&W Publications (2001)

---

For more information about the 72 Angels tradition, the Tree of Life, and Birth Angels with Terah Cox:
www.72BirthAngels.com

For permissions, additional works and information about author:
www.terahcox.com

# Table of Contents

# Gratitudes

Throughout the writing of the *Book of Days* five-volume series, which now includes this second revised edition of Volume 1, I have intimately experienced how much it truly does "take a village" of family, friends, colleagues and beyond to do our work and purposes in this world. The ongoing vibrancy of interaction among the "Angelic muses," readers and myself has given this journey a magical quality of co-creativity and sharing unlike anything I've ever experienced. The fact that this first volume is already being updated is a testament as to how dynamic my relationship has been with the material, my inner co-creators and the deepening of my own awareness and clarity.

First, I want to thank especially those whose friendship, multi-level support and feedback have been invaluable throughout the birthing of the whole series: My close friend and colleague, Stacie Florer, who has accompanied and encouraged me throughout the project, contributing so much through our co-creative conversations and her artistic and technical expertise; her mom, Paula Mooney for continually gracious feedback and support; close friends Jodi Tomasso and Chuck Pisa for their sharp insights and knowledge, Lindy Labriola for her raised-bar brilliance and our incredible thought-provoking conversations, Sara Labriola and my dear friend Teri Barr for helping me to keep it real, and the inimitable Donna Zucchi for reconnecting! Also thanks to all the Labriolas and the Delzells for the ongoing comfort of their friendship.

I'm also grateful to these and so many more for their participation in a crowdfunding campaign that helped to launch the project, as well as for contributions of stories, opinions and review blurbs, for feedback on the Daily Wisdoms via email, and for all whose continual support in different and generous ways afforded me the love, encouragement and time that I needed to birth this whole baby! ....

Aletheia Mystea, Annie Shaw, Arnie Roman & Tanya Leah, Barbara Lane, Beth Askew, Beth Smith, Cathleen O'Connor, Chuck Pisa, Cindy Cox, Claudia Duchene, Connie Hicks, Cornelius Chan, Dan Koppel, Davina Long, Dominic Petrillo, Dorothy Trottier, Eleonora Kouvoutsaki, Elizabeth Lehman, Elizabeth Hepburn, Ephrem Holdener, Fan Michail Anurag, Gilberto Costa, Go Ming Oi, Honey Kirila, Imogene Drummond, Isobel Stamford, Janice Tuchinsky, Jean Marzollo, Jodi

Tomasso, Jose Ramos, Joyce Byrum, Judith Clements, Kelly Klamut, Kerry-Fleur Schleifer, Laura Gould, Laura Parisi, Leiola Reeder, Lindy Labriola, Linda Wheeler Bryant, Loretta Melancon, Maria Macias, Marc Sabin, Mary Gracely, Michael Anastas, Paula Mooney, Paxton and Michael McAbee, Rebecca Mitchell, Reina Pinel, Sara Labriola, Sarah Gallant, Sharon Etienne, Stacie & Shayne Florer, Stacy Labriola, Stephanie Lodge, Stephanie Sulger, Sue Heiferman, Teresa Peppard, Teri Barr, Tina Wettengel, Yuta Kubareva.

I also want to express my deep gratitude to Linda Wheeler Bryant in Madrid, Spain for all her valuable input, and also for putting me in touch with the adult children of Kabaleb (Enrique Llop, 1927-1991), who was instrumental in resurrecting the medieval tradition of the 72 Angels in the 20th century. Kabaleb's children are carrying on their father's legacy through their own work and with additional publications of their father's works. I am so grateful for the help from Milena Llop (www.redmilenaria.com), Soleika Llop (www.alchemiagenetica.com.es), and Kabaleb's son, Tristan Llop (www.nuevavibracion.com), who spent hours with me via Skype to clarify the contributions of their father's work. This helped me to piece together some of the history of influences and certain aspects of the tradition that I had been seeking to understand more about for years (see Appendix II). *Muchas gracias y abrazos!!!*

Finally, I thank my family for understanding my hermiting needs over the course of this project: Cindy Cox, Connie Hicks, Bekah Hicks and Hannah, Aramis and Aden Zeno, Bill Juett, Dorothy Trottier and those who have departed but still remain in my heart.

There are many others who have supported my writing time through patronage in other aspects of my work from coaching to poetry art offerings and more, and sometimes through channels that don't enable me to know who you are. But please know how much your support has meant.

I am more and more filled with the awareness and gratitude for how much each of us matter – and that it is how we can share and inspire each other with what is inside us that really does give all our matter *mattering*! Thanks to all of you who have shared with me some of your own within, which has accompanied me, and this work, to this present moment with a full heart.

*Terah,* March 2015

*Love*

*does not ask you*

*to get out of the way*

*to bring something*

*'higher' through you.*

*Love invites you*

*to become*

*the way.*

*For the*

*higher*

*is already*

*within you.*

# Preface

*How this work came about*

This 5-volume year-long series represents my deepening co-creative work with the 72 Angels since the publication of the first *Birth Angels* book in 2004. *Birth Angels Book of Days* is a labor of love and a call to our willingness to "come within and receive." I had been feeling that I needed to update the original book with my new research and deeper understandings over the years of working with the tradition. But something different was coming forward from within me, and one day I heard, "*give the light a voice.*" Connecting this with other "inner tuitions," I felt that I must present the Angels in a different light and from a different angle – indeed, as "angles" of Divine Light within us – given to amplify our unique soul-light and help us to magnify and express the love and truth of who we are.

I was first drawn to the Kabbalah, from which the 72 Angels tradition emerged, because many of the truths at the heart of its mysticism had been spoken within me my whole life – especially after my initial spiritual awakening with a deeply loving Christic presence many years ago. Not affiliated with any church or religion – having thrown God out with the "Bible-belt bathwater" when I was kid – I was suddenly catapulted into a number of undeniable experiences which opened my heart to awareness of the Divine and a whole new inner life.

This led to years of inner teachings and communications waking and sleeping – including the instruction to explore not only the Bible, but also the holy books of other traditions. In doing so, I became fascinated with the sameness at the heart of so many religions and paths despite their wide range of vocabularies, creeds and cultures. Eventually, all my multi-traditional and inner explorations showed me a beautiful paradox of life – that our diversity has a sacred purpose, and at the same time, "*all roads lead home for any heart willing to come.*" It seems that we are so loved in our humanity that

"Truth" meets us wherever and whoever we are – and that it *enjoys* whatever creed, language, ritual, path or soapbox we choose – as long as the *Love* at its heart is conveyed.

While continuing to explore the different paths and ways, one morning an instruction was given to me inwardly which would impact my spiritual journey from that moment on: "*Let not my words from the saintliest lips or the holiest books come before my Word at the altar of your own heart.*" I suppose I could have taken that as a cue to start my own cult (!) – but being who I am instead of who I'm not, I knew I was being called to a deeper personal "response-ability" to measure what was coming from the outside against my own within. It was, essentially, about putting the inner Divine first.

As a lifelong seeker of the resonances of truth wherever I could find them, I understood that my every quest from then on must start and end in the truth of my own heart and soul. For in this way I might understand what parts of the "I AM" that I am here to express through the isness and truths of my own being and life-purposing. Furthermore, by looking out at the world through this inner Divine "lens," I could see my fellow beings in a whole new light.

But there was something missing in my understanding of truth that I wouldn't get until years later. In the meantime, Truth – the trickster and shapeshifter that it often is – led me down many winding roads and off-roads, rattling my resistant inner cages of pride and doubt, always seeking the heart of the matter or the person, teaching me to listen to not only what was said, but what longed to be. I didn't realize that slowly, gently, crazily and passionately, truth itself was teaching me its most important lesson of all: that *no truth can be a whole Truth without the all-seeing transformative Love that reveals what only Love can see.*

And so, ultimately I saw that the "truer-truth," or "whole truth" – which I now understand as Love and Truth commingled – includes rather than excludes, unites rather than divides, and illuminates our worthiness rather than instilling shame or doubt.

This is because the whole truth knows our whole story, which includes the longing in our hearts to love and be loved, to know and be more of who we truly are and to give something good and worthwhile to this world.

By the Angelic "inroads" paved through me, I began to grasp the deeper meanings in the sayings of Jesus and others throughout the ages who have come to show us that the Divine is not separate from us, but *within* us. And to consider that the Christic energy is woven into the fabric of our souls as our "image and likeness" to the Divine, only needing our recognition. And I saw the 72 Angels as awakeners within us of the Divine "love-in-detail" by which we might be personally attended to in our days and hours of challenge and potential.

In the 72 Angels tradition, the Angel that corresponds to the day works within the human heart, and I realized that the *Book of Days* idea came to me as a way to bring more awareness, love and truth into our daily lives and relationships. The Wisdoms set our awareness and offer us a deeper daily immersion into our hearts as the vantage point from which we may experience and interact with the world. When our awareness is alive and crackling, it acts like a magnet to draw learning and loving experiences and to show us the magical interconnectivity of life.

Ultimately, as the Angels say, Divine-self realization is not a matter of "*getting out of the way,*" but rather "*becoming the way.*" Nor is it about what we must *do* to become "more spiritual," but rather to allow our awareness of who we *are*, truly and deeply, emerge and expand. Always, the Wisdoms remind us that it is "*the softer, receptive side of will that is willingness*" which brings us into the full power of our Divine-Human beingness.

The co-creating of the Wisdoms has been a transformative leg on my own inner journey as each day's writing has become my daily practice of communion with the Divine. As all five volumes of the Daily Wisdoms have now been published, I am in the process of editing them again because of the deepening understandings that have emerged along the way. As my life and work continue to teach me, knowing is only one part of the journey; it is a whole other thing for knowledge to be transformed into wisdom and the ability to BE what we can know – and it is a continually renewed awareness which achieves that.

"Being" happens in the small moments when we aren't thinking or worrying about yesterday or tomorrow, when we feel a surge of joy for the recognition of what's right in front of us or inside us. Or when we suddenly let the notion of who we *should* be slip away to the relief of accepting who we are. Being. That's what work with the Angels, and any spiritual path that invites transformation, calls us to – the willingness to be present and allow the inner wonders within us to emerge in their own time.

In the meantime, as the Angel HAHAHEL says, "*you do not have to have arrived at your destination to point the way to a fellow traveler.*" And so here are these words, hopefully conveying the love that brought them forth, and here you are reading and receiving. And there you likely are in your life, sharing in your own way what you know and feel as you come to it. And though this work is given from one who has not yet arrived at her destination, I am on the journey. As are you, as are all. And as long as our journeys include the inner terrains, I trust we're going somewhere that matters.

# Introduction

*Looking at the Angels in a different light*

---

Through the ages, Angels have been in the religious histories, spiritual experiences, imagination, literature and art of humankind as Divine messengers, guardians and guides. However, the 20th century brought the resurgence of a long-hidden medieval Angelic tradition within the Judaic Kabbalah which revealed a much deeper role of certain Angels as aspects of the Divine Itself, which express and amplify the Divine within humanity. With connections to the earliest known Kabbalah oral traditions and texts, the 12th century work of Rabbi Yitzhak Ha-Ivver (Isaac the Blind) in Provence, France (c. 1160–1235) on the Tree of Life and the 72 Angels was further developed by his student Rabbi Moses ben Nahman (Nachmanides, or RaMBaN) (1194-1270) and other Rabbis and multi-traditional mystics and scholars into 13th-15th century Gerona, Spain. In 1492 the Judaic school and grotto were walled up and abandoned during the Conversion/Expulsion Edict of the Spanish Inquisition in which Jews were forced to convert to Christianity, face death or flee. Many fled to Safed, Israel, where in the 16th century Rabbis Moshes Cordovero and Isaac Luria are credited with detailing the symbology of the Tree of Life and its Angelic aspects. Over the next few centuries certain Europeans would pick up the "Angelic baton," notably Lazare Lenain in the 19th century, who did further work with the 72 Angels and their esoteric astrological correspondences and qualities.

In the late 1970's and 80's, a "gentrification" trend in Gerona spurred excavations of the medieval grotto and school, which brought about the discovery and research of hidden Hebrew parchments. In the meantime, Gerona journalist and Kabbalah scholar Enrique Llop (writing as Kabaleb) had begun his work with the 72 Angels and esoteric astrology, augmenting the work of Lenain and drawing from the lineage of Isaac the Blind. He also worked with renowned 20th century Kabbalist Omraam Mikhaël Aïvanhov (1900-1986), who lectured extensively on the mysteries of bringing the Kingdom of God to Earth within the individual through the mysteries of the Christ and aspects of Esoteric Christianity. Kabaleb's works were published in France under the name of his longtime friend Haziel. Today, Kabaleb's legacy is carried on by his adult children, Tristan, Milena and Soleika Llop. I invite you to explore "Appendix II" for more details on the Llop family, Kabbalah cosmology and the development of the 72 Angels tradition from the 12th-21st centuries.

The illuminations of the 72 Angels tradition reveal that the roles of the Angels in the cosmos and in human life are much deeper and more intricately woven into our lives than most of us have ever realized. I have spent years off and on researching the "provenance" and aspects of the tradition and the similarities of its central themes to other traditions. But my growing interest, and the purpose of this work, is focused more on daily practice and the dynamics of direct communion with the Divine through the Angelic energies which express particularities of Its nature within the particularities of our human nature.

As I neared the completion of the first edition of the *Book of Days* series, I began to coalesce the themes and threads running through the Daily Wisdoms. Probably the foundational message is one that has been conveyed to us for thousands of years from the mystical hearts of many traditions and individual spiritual sojourns. This message is that the Divine dwells within us, even as we dwell within the Divine. And thus we are not only human, but Divine-Human beings. As such, we have the power of direct communion with the Divine through our heart and soul and the greater totality of Spirit which these give us access to.

The difficulty we may have with embracing the idea of "the Divine within us" is on several levels. First, we have been indoctrinated for centuries with (a) the idea of a separate, fearsome God that dwells *outside* of us, somewhere 'up there,' above and beyond us, even judging us, and that (b) we are all sinners incapable of saving our puny, temptable flesh without the God that has been prescribed to us – which has rooted in us a secret sense of shame from which no amount of good works can ever quite redeem us.

And then there's (c): we are often most blind to what is right in front of us and inside us, and thus (d) we play our lives out and exercise our consciousness through outer relationships. We project the issues of our own psyches onto others, as they do upon us – and if we're smart enough to realize that we're blaming other people for our own stuff, then we learn and grow from the mirrors we provide for each other. If not, we just keep doing the same things over and over until something happens that wakes us up (thanks to the subterranean work of our soul)! Living our lives in the dynamics of otherness is natural and deeply-ingrained when you consider that we come to this Earth to individuate through the contrast and complement that relationship provides.

And we can take this even deeper. If we are truly made "in the image and likeness of God," then we must consider the possibility that we are here because of the desire of the Divine Itself to experience life and relationship and what more it might become through the individuations and creations of Its own creations. Thus, seen in this light, we are Divinely urged to create our lives with and in the presence of "otherness."

The Daily Wisdoms address all of this by giving the Angelic lights a voice for our time. Here, the 72 Angels invite us into a dynamic relationship with the "Other" *within* us – so that we might become wholly and fully human – empowered to achieve our full potential on Earth by virtue of our inner Divine "soul-spark." Thereby the Divine may experience life through each of us, and as us, in the unique ways, being and doing of our particular preferences and purposes. "The Kingdom of Heaven is within," Jesus told us. "All I do you can do and more."

I became acutely aware during the writing of this series that the primary key to truly grasping the concept that we are Divine-Human beings is: **awareness**. That's what starts the spiritual alchemy of turning our base human *mettle* into Divine-Human gold. To repeat this from the Preface: When our awareness is alive and crackling, it acts like a magnet to draw learning and loving experiences and to show us the magical interconnectivity of life. Through daily and moment-to-moment renewal of awareness, over time we come to feel our human substance, thoughts, feelings, attitudes, choices and behaviors transformed and ennobled.

Throughout the co-creating of these works with the Angelic "others" within me, I have often received outer confirmation of what I was being given inwardly. In the last couple of days of editing Volume 5, I happened upon two lectures – one with Andrew Harvey (www.TheShiftNetwork.com), and another with Deepak Chopra in a special for public television. Uncannily the message of both was the same – that the "time is upon us when we must realize that the Divine is within," and that we are charged with the "divinization" of our humanity in order to "save the soul of our world." Harvey, who works with "The Christpath" and "Sacred Activism," actually used the term "divine human" again and again! And Chopra talked about how important our awareness is in embodying "the Divine within." In fact, the PBS fundraiser bonus was Chopra's "The Divine Within Collection!" These are constant themes in all five volumes of the *Book of Days*. So I think we're onto something here!

# The Mysteries of the Divine

---

In attempting to part the veil on the Divine mysteries, it has been suggested to us by scholars and mystics through the ages that if we are indeed "made in the image and likeness of God," as some of our oldest spiritual literatures claim, then we can know God if we come to know ourselves.

## *"Know Thyself"*

The way of coming to know God by deeper knowledge of our own humanity has been echoed throughout the centuries by spiritual explorers, mystics, poets and artists seeking to know who we are and why we are compelled as we are in life. Rumi, Hafiz, Yogananda, Lao Tzu, William Blake, Walt Whitman, and many more come to mind. The Greek oracle at Delphi said, "Know Thyself." Pythagorus (6th c.) said it more fully: "Man, know thyself; then thou shalt know the Universe and God." Christian mystic and theologian Jacob Boehme proposed in the 16th century that our inner human qualities are "signatures" of the Divine Itself within and among us when he said, "God's mysteries can be only known by God, and to know them we must first seek God in our own center." (www.jacobboehmeonline.com). In 1831 Ralph Waldo Emerson wrote a poem entitled "Know Thyself" (transl.) on the theme of the God within that exists in all. And then there are the Biblical sayings, "...God created mankind in his own image" (Genesis 1:27), or "...the Word of the Lord created man in his likeness (John 1:1), "...on Earth as it is in Heaven (Lord's Prayer); and the Hermetic Emerald Tablet: "That which is Below is like to that which is Above."

Those who do not believe in the concept of a God – or at least the God that mainstream religions have historically proffered – have sometimes accused man of creating God in his own image, from our own need or desperation, or in not wanting to be responsible for our own circumstances, etc. And that may be at least partially true –

especially when God has been depicted as a fearsome, angry, rigid, judging or indifferent God who is a "spitting image" of all those "lower" qualities in our own nature. But doesn't it make more sense that if we are made in the image and likeness of the Divine, it would be as our "higher," more noble qualities that are the constant life-affirming aspirations in all of humankind, no matter what our ideologies?

**The "mark of the Maker."** Inherent within all of us, as if we are hard-wired to them, are these central lifelong preoccupations around which our whole lives are played out: (1) the longing for belonging, meaning and purpose, which spurs (2) the desire to love and be loved, (3) the desire to know who, what and why we are, which causes us (4) to seek ourselves in each other and in our own creations, and (5) to give something worthwhile to the world from what we love and who we truly are. Thus you might say that these deepest urges in our nature are as inner "imprints" or microcosmic echoes of the very nature of our origin – the "mark of the Maker" within Its creations.

Another clue to the pervasiveness of the Divine Nature within and around us is in the movements and cycles that propel life – the same movements of contraction and expansion that are said to have brought about Creation and which scientists agree propel the universes and life at all levels. We experience these movements in our life-supporting functions such as breath in-breath out, the two in-and-out pulses that compose a heartbeat, the labors of birthing and the cycles of life, death and rebirth, the ebb and flow of the tides and the dying and rebirthing seasons of the natural world. In all life forms, the cycle is echoed and repeated: Life comes into being, moves toward fulfillment and fruition, peaks, wanes, builds up energetic conditions and momentum for return, and in due time rebirths its essence into new forms.

**Parting the veil.** Some years ago I began to consider what was happening *before* "the Beginning," why Creation came about, and what was the initial impulse that propelled it? But these are not new questions. Humankind has been wondering and contemplating about these and more from at least the beginning of recorded history – and using clues from the natural world and our own human nature to seek existential understanding of our origin, meaning and purpose. Indeed, every culture on Earth has a creation story, many of which are similar. I think if we truly want to know something, the "Universe" answers us – and it's up to us to hear and sometimes decode the answer. Because the Divine seems to meet us where we are, answers often come in vocabularies and contexts that are already familiar to us, but which we must perhaps look at "in a different light" – beyond the paradigms of commonly accepted beliefs and perspectives.

From the beginning of my own experiences with the Christic mysteries and uncanny inner tuitions that would be given to me through dreams, visions and inwardly audible teachings, I have been prompted to look at everything in a different light. Thus I considered many of the biblical stories, the sayings of Jesus and others differently from standard theological interpretations. When I was led to the 72 Angels tradition, I was somewhat intrigued, though I had never been drawn to the new age presentations of angels. I kept trying to walk away from working with this tradition, but I kept being pulled back in – and then deeper and deeper in until I was ready to see the Angels in a different light.

One early morning just on the cusp of dreaming and waking, I had this vision:

> I saw a great white light, alive and pulsing like a heartbeat, and I felt its tremendous longing to know what it was made of. Then there was a welling up of feeling that was so much more than the word love could encompass. Suddenly the white light shattered and exploded outward into a glorious array of colors and sounds and energies. Over that spectacular landscape the word "Angels" appeared, and then the "e" and "l" transposed so that the word spelled "Angles."

This signaled a different perspective, a different "angle" (pun intended) on the Angels, and the Divine Itself, that I wouldn't begin to grasp until years later. As I continued to research, study and write about this tradition through the years, I felt I have been always dancing between the worlds of accepted knowledge and my own mystical experiences and inner tuitions. But then that is how the Kabbalah itself, which means "the receiving," was developed. And indeed, all humanity's great religions were founded and continually propelled by mystical experiences. The very act of creating is often a mystical experience! It perhaps cannot be known whether mystical experiences and teachings are meant to be literal or symbolic, but when they become concretized by dogma and tradition they tend to lose their fluidity, inclusiveness and the dynamics of love within them that reveal the greater truths.

And so, in my own work, I try to use traditional perspectives to help organize the mystical input, and the mystical work to re-enliven and shine new light on established paradigms and ways of thinking. While what follows is as simple a rendering as I can muster of the very complex Kabbalah cosmology, it is not necessary to take it in or understand it in order to engage dynamically with the Angels. I offer it here because this first volume symbolizes our Source, our cosmic soul-birth and our ongoing relationship with the Divine within our own humanity.

The next four volumes are more "down to Earth!" – I promise!

## ***The Self-birthing of the Divine into the Cosmos***

Medieval Kabbalists used the symbology of the Tree of Life to explain the levels of the Divine Self-Emanation and Revelation which would ultimately bring about Creation. Kabbalists attribute to 16$^{th}$ century Rabbi Moshe Cordovero and Rabbi Isaac Luria of Safed, Israel, the most comprehensive and detailed systematizing of Kabbalah creation cosmology which had been started by 12$^{th}$ century Isaac the Blind. Their "mapping" of the Tree of Life shows that the Divine Light began to emanate from an unknowable and undifferentiated "No-Thingness" into and through the "Four Worlds of Existence" (World of Emanation, World of Creation, World of

Formation and World of Action) and the "vessels" of the Ten Sephirot of the Tree, in order to reveal the differentiated aspects of Itself. (See "The Kabbalah Tree of Life" quick-reference chart at 72BirthAngels.com)

This is a complex tradition, so I offer a brief summary with some sense of hierarchy in order to give some background to the similarities between the Divine and human nature, and how the 72 Angels were said to emerge. I've also interjected some questions and possible connecting of cosmic dots that have come through the Angel wisdoms and other inner teachings.

The very top of the Tree glyph begins "before the beginning" with a progression of the Divine as it emanated from the "Three Veils of Negative Existence" – (1) the "Ain," (2) the "Ain Sof," and then finally (3) the "Ain Sof Aur" – down through the Tree and out into what would ultimately become Creation.

**1-No-Thingness**. The "Ain" (also Ayn or Ein), which means *No-Thing*, describes the infinite No-thingness of the Unknowable and Undifferentiated Void. Kabbalah creation cosmology says that before "the Beginning," All was God and God was All and One, and there was nothing that was not God. But because there was only the One, God was not knowable, even to Itself. A kind of "sleeping cosmic giant," so to speak.

**2-No-Thingness Without End**. This is the "Ain Sof," which refers to the Divine without name or manifestation or any attribute which would impose definition or limitation. Here it is thought that the Divine began to become aware of the existence and vastness of Itself, but yet without thought, form or knowableness to any other, because there was no other.

**2B-Movement**. This would have been happening between the second and third "Veils," when there must have arisen from within the "No-Thingness Without End" an urge, or stirring of **desire**, which Kabbalists say is the "motor of the Universe." This desire created movement – the first of which was **withdrawal**, or

**contraction** of Itself (what Kabbalah calls the "Tzimtzum") – in order to create a space void of Itself so that there would be a space to receive Itself. During the withdrawal, which caused the compression of Its energy and essence, a momentum built which finally erupted into a burst of outward **expansion**. This represents the birthing of the Divine from the womb of Its own darkness.

Interestingly, this is echoed in humankind as the first contraction that begins the labors of birthing of a child. But in the birthing of the Divine, what was the motivating and propelling desire that caused the first contraction? This is where I am particularly moved to resource ancient knowledge, the laws of movement in the cosmos, the nature of man and what I have understood through the Angel Wisdoms. If from within the great vastness arose the primordial birth of desire, I propose that the desire of the Divine was this: **to know what It was**. And then, there arose from Its desire something from within It to fulfill the desire. I propose that it was what the Angel Wisdoms call **the creation energy of Love**, which would propel outward the "I AM" that the Divine was, in order to reveal Its true nature. In a similar way, we humans are compelled to know who we are – and as we discover our personal truths, a desire to express them wells up within us.

And so, is it possible that the essential nature of what Kabbalists (and many other traditions) perceive as the Father-Mother God, might be Truth and Love? Is it during this stage of Divine Self-Revelation where It began to be knowable and relatable to Itself in Its two-fold nature? Would this then be the Divine realization of inner "Otherness" and the cosmic template of "two within one" and "one-becomes-two" that would ultimately be imprinted and imaged within the manifestation of Creation as masculine/truth and feminine/love?

**3- No-Thingness With Never Ending Light** is the "Ain Sof Aur," which is said to have brought forth sound and light simultaneously with "Let there be Light!" This first "Divine

Utterance" utilized the movements of contraction (breath in) and expansion (breath out) that would bring forth the light that would propel life, what both Judaism and Christianity call "the Word." Here began the Divine Emanation as Light into the cosmos.

I am curious about relating the concept of the Christ to this stage of Divine Emanation, which is described by John 1.1 of the New Testament as: "...even that Word that was in the beginning with God, and was God, and in time became incarnate, by whom all things were made." Could the emergence of the Christic "Word" be seen as the "Light-child" of the Father-Mother God? And would this perhaps explain the reference in the Angel Wisdoms to the Light as the child of the commingling of Love and Truth? Perhaps I presume too much, but these are interesting questions and may at least point to possible dynamics of the Divine mysteries in aspects of our humanity.

**4-Emanation of the Light**. Here the Divine Light, as yet undifferentiated, begins to radiate out into the cosmos. It is important here to consider the difference between "emanation" and "creation." Emanation is the exuding or radiating of a vibratory energy from its source. We commonly refer to this in our human relatings as an energy or "vibe" someone "gives off" that conveys a quality of feeling or attitude. Creation, however, involves the duality of essence AND the physicality of matter. While as created beings we contain the energy and essence of our Source in, and as, our soul, it is encased within a denser structure of substances that compose the matter of our bodies and give our soul "a leg to stand on." All living things in Creation have this dual nature of essence and form.

With the first emanation of Light, the Divine is still indistinguishable because the otherness expressed by Its own two-fold nature is still hidden within it. But as the Light continues to emanate, that will change.

**5-Differentiation of the Divine Self.** Here the emanating Divine Light was differentiated into aspects and qualities of Itself, with the Sephirotic vessels acting as "prisms." It is during this stage where it is said that the Divine became knowable as what the ancients call the "Angels of the Presence," which came forth on the "first day" and were said to represent "the faces of God, as God Itself." These were perceived by Kabbalists as the 72 Angels which reveal "the 72-Lettered Name and Qualities of God," ultimately filling nine of the Ten Sephirot on the Tree. And thusly, the Divine Light was "refracted" into 72 "angles" of light, as Angelic hues and aspects – perhaps akin to the refraction of white light into visible colors through the mechanism of a prism. The Light/light is not divided, because it is indivisible; rather it is simply revealed.

Rabbi Cordovero's view, as presented here, would seem to concur...

> ...[like] how water poured into differently-shaped vessels will take on the vessels' forms, or how light streaming through different colors of glass appears in different colors. Despite the change in appearance, the water and the light emanate from a single source and are essentially unchanged; the vessels merely serve to filter and veil the light to reveal different aspects of the Creator, and to permit creations to benefit from His Light. http://en.wikipedia.org/wiki/Ein_So

Thus, it is through the "refraction" of Divine Light into the 72 Angels of the Sephirotic vessels that the Divine expressed Itself as definable aspects of both quantity and quality: Its *quantifiable* existence as I AM, i.e., Truth (number and form) and *qualifiable* expansion of Its I AM into I AM THAT WHICH, through Love (essence and meaning). These aspects of quantity and quality would ultimately be conveyed into all of Creation as the image and likeness of the Divine in, and as, innumerable variations and diversities of form and meaning. There are also schools of Kabbalah thought which say that the Angels themselves were invested with the power of creation, because as emanated aspects of the Divine they would therefore express those same powers.

According to the earliest known text revealing Kabbalah creation cosmology, the "Sefer Yetzirah" (Book of Formation, or Creation), the cosmos and all the worlds were created with sound and light.

The Divine Sounds, which named the qualities of the Divine as it "spilled forth" and "cascaded" down through the Sephirotic vessels of the Tree, are shown on the Tree as the 22 spiraling Paths that connect the Sephirot (in the same spiral formation as human DNA). These 22 Sounds ultimately became ascribed as the 22 letters of the Hebrew Alphabet.

The Tree of Life also symbolizes "Adam Kadmon," as Universal Man, said to express the paradox of humanity as the "manifestation of Primordial Divinity" (which supports the concept of the "Divine-Human being"). The architecture of these cosmic worlds and all their aspects are viewed by Kabbalists as the template for Creation and the Divine within man.

**6-Dispersion of the Light**. There is another part of this creation cosmology introduced by Lurianic Kabbalah which may add some explanation, and certainly complexity, into the accounts of how Creation came about. Rabbi Luria, supported by certain passages in the Bible's Genesis and Chronicles, postulated that the "intensity" of the light as it continued to descend down the Tree into the Sephirotic vessels caused the "shattering of the vessels," dispersing the Differentiated Light of the Divine Essence as the "shards" of the vessels broke. As they fell from the heavens toward the Worlds of Creation, Formation and Action, each retained the essence, powers and likeness of that which came before it, all "echoing" the original Source, the Divine Itself, in the ability to create, expand and self-perpetuate – though in diluted degrees.

Lurianic Kabbalah says, however, that the shattering of the vessels ultimately created a "weaker" stream of light, and thus an imperfect world was created. From this, the concept of "Tikun" or "Tikkun Olam" came about, which says that all of humankind is charged with the rectification and repair of the world. Perhaps this echoes the Angel Wisdoms which speak of responsibility for our world and the necessity for every generation to heal the hurts of our time, as well as any residue of the past.

**7-The birth of Creation**. The ultimate purpose of Creation was said to be the rootedness of the heavens upon Earth and the manifestation of the Divine within humanity and all of Creation. Through the Divine soul-spark incarnated within the physical matter of humankind, the ever-expanding Divine Potential could be manifested throughout the cosmos and infinity, and the inherent diversity of Its Oneness expressed in, and as, the diversity of all beings and things.

**The two-way dynamics between the Divine and the Human**. As discussed earlier, the Tree of Life is a glyph for Divine Emanation and Creation and a template for the "implant" of the Divine within mankind. It is also a map for the two-way exchange between the Divine and the Human in the dynamics of our inner-outer being. As the Divine Essence expresses Itself through our physicality, whatever we manifest through the uniqueness of our humanity reverberates in our inner Divine. As our humanity becomes more awake to the Divine within us, we ascend in consciousness to the higher realms of the Tree, as the saturation and commingling of the Divine within our humanity.

As the Kabbalah and other ageless wisdoms agree, the Divine Itself, and our relationship with It, is not fixed or governed by immutable law. In the ongoing two-way exchange of energy and information that is carried on the cosmic currents of Love and Truth between the Divine and the Human, both the Divine and the Human are affected. While the Divine is said to be "Absolute" in Its I AM, this does not mean It is fixed or unchanging. The Divine is dynamic – movement is integral to the full expression of Its nature, just as it is within life and all beings. Thus, just as we are affected and evolved by our experiences of the Divine interacting with us, so is the Divine affected and evolved by us and all we think, feel, do and become.

# The Mysteries of Humanity

## *The Inner and Outer of Us*

Pretty much all spiritual paths and traditions agree, in their different vocabularies, that we humans are walking-talking-thinking-feeling dualities composed of inner and outer aspects: **essence** (soul) and **form** (body/personality). Body and personality constitute our outer interface with the world. Composed of the stuff of Earth, including oxygen, carbon, hydrogen, nitrogen, calcium, and phosphorus, our body has a much denser vibration than our essence and constitutes the matter and form that, again, gives our soul literal legs to stand on. Our personalities, simply put, are our outer behavioral expressions, the persona which we fashion as our outer mask. Together our body and our personality creates a separateness of space in which we may individuate and explore our unique potentials. In this space we exercise our choices of how we will express our inner being through love and self-realization in ways that will play out in the contrast and complement of relationship.

The foundation of our invisible inner realm is our soul, said to be a spark of the Divine Itself, holding within its potential a particular constellation of Divine light-qualities which we are deeply urged to express in physical life. It is the soul which carries our inner image and likeness of the Divine, animates our body and gives our life meaning and purpose. Our whole life we are in a continual exchange between our inner and outer, with our primary "directive" coming from the inner – our soul-urges and purposes, which are broadcast into our hearts and translated as our intuitions, spiritual longings and personal heart-truths. These are always striving to be acknowledged and expressed outwardly, even while inviting us to bring our outer experiences inward to make sense and meaning of them.

We often forget or suppress aspects of our softer, more diffuse, inner nature in the demands of our daily lives and the needs and preoccupations of the physical vehicle that is our interface with the world. As the Angel Wisdoms acknowledge, we become much consumed by the responsibilities, pleasures and challenges of the visible outer world – while our inner realms can sometimes seem like a "*swampy soup of feelings, thoughts and desires*" that we often put off sorting out. As the Angels show us, however, the great paradox of ourselves as Divine-Human beings is that the more we awaken to and engage with our inner divinity, the more empowered and wholly human we can become.

**Why are we here?** As Divine-Human beings, we have the lifelong paradoxical challenge to draw from the unlimited potential imprinted within us while in the seeming limitations of flesh and Earth-life! Why, you might ask, as we have been asking probably from the beginning of time. Why are we here in this foreign outpost where we have to walk-not-fly, with eyes veiled, inner ears deafened, true self muffled and mostly forgetful of everything we already know, to muddle through this obstacle course of becoming that which we already are?

As this question lingered within me, one Spring morning I was walking in a Hudson Highlands forest of upstate New York admiring all the newborn life around me when I began to "hear" these words. I sat on a stone wall to capture them on paper....

> *You are the farthest reaches of the Divine's desire to know what more it is made of and what more it might become through your own makings. The one thing the Divine cannot experience without you is limitation. You are the 'Way' for the experience of creation in the context of seeming limits, even as the Divine Itself is the Way for you to live a more wholly-human life that is 'super-charged' by the Divine qualities imprinted within you. As you branch out into your world, the Divine with its inherent urge to increase, flower and come to fruition branches out toward the light with you, for you and as you. It is what you call a win-win for both the Divine and the Human, for there are potentials of Life and Love and Truth*

*that can only be expressed through physicality and matter. You are the way the Heart and Mind of God may be known and increased. You are the way Heaven comes to Earth.*

As the retelling here takes me back to that moment, I am flooded again with awe and humility. We are not ever "*only human*." On this Earth we are the all of it – both Divine and Human – expressing howevermuch of either or both of those we choose to express in any moment of time. I love the possibilities in this paradox that we are! Yes, Earth life seems to pull us toward the denser vibrations of matter – but it is the heart and soul within us that shows us which matter really does *matter* to us! And it does seem that the more we allow our inner to weigh in with our outer choices and expressions, the lighter and more fulfilled we become. And the more our relationships and creations flower with light and meaning, the more love and wisdom is rooted within and among us.

**Our Love-and-Truth Nature**. Our lifelong urges to love and be loved and to know the truth of who we are seem to be woven into the very fabric of our inner being, even as physicality is to our bodies. And so if we are made in the image and likeness of the Divine, then there must be a connection between these urges within our own nature and the nature of the Divine Itself.

The Angel wisdoms tell us that truth in human beingness represents the nature and qualities of our personal I Am – our existential "isness" – which echoes that part of the Divine I AM which we are here to embody and express. But something has to move the isness of who we are, other than will or intellect (we all know how far we get with those on our diets and exercise routines). Our isness, our truths, must be ignited by something much more compelling. And so we have love. Love is not just a feeling. It signals and propels our meaning and purpose. It is the creation energy that expands, evolves and moves the truth of who we are out into the world for expression.

Between the two, love is more universally recognizable and pretty much unarguable (except maybe when we're not being loved the way we want) – whereas through the ages we have fought wars and killed and conquered whole tribes and nations over our different and very possessive notions of Truth. But alas for the myriad proponents of an "only" Truth, there continue to be as many hues and expressions of Truth as there are those seeking and proclaiming it!

I think it likely that there is no only-Truth on Earth, as badly as we or any of our religious traditions may we want to cling to ownership of one. Because our diversity reflects and expresses the inherent diversity of the Divine Oneness – Truth, as the Divine I AM, has many relative paths and vocabularies in life. Thus Truth is, paradoxically, both absolute and relative: absolute as the totality of the Divine, but relative in its multitude of expressions through Creation. The full power of Truth, however, is not unleashed until it is in the company of Love.

A lover of truth my whole life, I was led to understand the importance of love at a whole other level in the spontaneous writing of a fable entitled *The Story of Love and Truth.* In this small poignant tale, Love and Truth are two halves of a pair, until one day Truth gets a notion to leave Love behind to see what adventures and glory it might find in the world on its own. Finally, after all the puffed up truth-telling havoc and hurt that the lone Truth eventually causes to itself and the world, Love leaves the safety of home to go in search of the missing Truth. In their dramatic reunion, in which Love rises to its own greater potential in order to save Truth from its fallen stature, they realize that neither of them can come into their fullness without the other. Truth declares to Love, "I, Truth, can know who beings are, but you can feel who they long to be. I was born to enlighten the world – but you Love, only you can change the world."

I have learned that, together with Love, Truth is responsive, fluid and always evolving – never fixed – meeting us exactly as what we are, not what we or someone else may think we *should* be. Because of Love and Truth we have an infinite number of second chances to awaken and express more and more of who we are. Because of Love and Truth, we seek and find ourselves in each other. Because of Love and Truth, which the Angel Wisdoms say brought forth the Light that sees all, we are always seen in our totality by the Divine, without judgment. And, because of Love and Truth commingled with and within us, we may become the more that we are within All That Is, born anew on Earth as a Divine-Human being.

## ***The Power of Heart***

In our quest for knowledge and the acquisition of more and more stuff, the incessant need to stay on the cutting edge and to keep up with the latest information and trends, we are often forgetting to consider what *meaning* any of it has for us – the what-and-who-matters-most that gives anything we do or achieve significance. The only way we can know that is through feeling and a sense of connection and purpose – and for that we need our hearts.

As the Angels in their heart-influence show us, the heart is the bridge between our inner and our outer: our heart-and-soul and our body-mind. Our heads cannot think our way through or undo all the "de-meaning" circumstances that fear, shame, pain, greed, power and hate cause to individuals, societies and the Earth itself. If we want to begin to heal ourselves and our world, and come into our *true* power, we must learn to lead with the heart – that part of us that holds the soul-memory of our eternal Divine nature and transforms knowledge and experience into wisdom and understanding...the part that expresses the graces of love, compassion and forgiveness within and among us...the part which reminds us that for all our outer differences we are mostly the same on the inside, wanting to love and be loved and live our lives with meaning and purpose from the truth of who we are.

As Gail Godwin explores in her book entitled *Heart*, almost every mystical system in the history of the world tells us that we may know the mind of the Divine through our hearts, and that our most potent and personal communication with the Divine is that which originates in our own hearts. Siddha Yoga guru Bhagawan Nityananda said, "The heart is the hub of all sacred places." In Hindu mysticism, the *Upanishads* (meaning "connection") "focus[es] on the God to be discovered [where it] already resides in the secret cave of our heart...the great fulcrum of the cosmos." (p. 43) Aryeh Kaplan suggests in his commentary on the *Sefir Yetzirah* that "it is in the heart that the action of [Divine] Mind is manifest in the body...and the heart serves as a causal link between mind and body. ...Therefore...the power of perception and the soul's ability to nourish itself must lie in the heart." (p. 76)

These all have even more resonance in the light of growing scientific research which challenges the long-held belief that the brain is the "master controller" of our bodily systems. As our technology has advanced, scientists have been able to measure the subtle electrical field of the heart as ranging far beyond that of the brain. Since 1991, the Institute of HeartMath has expanded upon the heart-brain research of physiologists John and Beatrice Lacey of the Fels Institute in the 1970's, neurocardiologist Dr. J. Andrew Armour in 1991, and other scientists and researchers, which show that the heart has its own "central intelligence system" – essentially a mind of its own. Research shows that the heart is a "causal" source which initiates messages to the brain and body via the nervous system, pulse waves, hormones and electromagnetics. Interestingly, the heart is auto-rhythmic – meaning the heartbeat is self-generating – and it is the first organ to develop in a human fetus. It is only after the first components of the developing heart appear (left and right endocardial tubes which are animated by an "electrical spark" of some kind, initiating the heartbeat and the rest of the formation of the heart), that the first part of the brain begins to develop, which is the emotional region – and the thinking region of the brain grows out of that. Another very striking fact noted in *The HeartMath Solution* (Doc Childre and Howard Martin with Donna Beech, HarperCollins 2000), is that while scientists concur that the brain controls the timing or pace of the heartbeat, "the heart doesn't need a hardwired connection to the brain to keep beating. For example, [after] a heart transplant, the nerves that run from the brain to the heart are severed, and surgeons don't know yet how to connect them. But that doesn't stop the heart from functioning. After surgeons have implanted a heart and restored its beat in a new person's chest, the heart keeps beating – though there's no longer any connection to a brain." (*The HeartMath Solution*, p. 9, and decryptedmatrix.com/live/intelligent-energy-thoughts-and-feelings-matter)

One has to wonder if the heart-prioritized order of fetal development is symbolically suggestive that we are meant to live *a heart-driven life*. This calls to mind one of my favorite "out of the mouth of babes" wisdoms from my older goddaughter Lindy when she was just 5. While in the car one day she suddenly asked me "how do babies get born?" "I'm sure your mommy and daddy will want to tell you all about that someday!" I told her. "No, I want you to tell me right now!" she insisted. So I skirted the explanation a little and went straight to the machine that could look inside the mommy's belly to see if there was a baby there. She got excited by that, and asked me what the machine could see. "The baby's heart beating," I replied. Her eyes got big, and then she thought a minute and said excitedly, "I know why that's the first thing they have to see – because if it didn't have a heart there would be no point for it be born because it wouldn't have anything to love people with!" Amen. Amazing how children know everything worth knowing before we start to teach them what we think they should know!

We often talk about our physical and emotional heart somewhat interchangeably, and debates about where exactly our emotional heart is located can be quite lively. Of course our physical heart is the organ in our chest that pumps blood throughout our body and which, if the newest science is correct, also sends signals and messages to our brain and body. But the intangible emotional heart – with its capacity for feeling and its "tiny voice" of intuition, wisdom and spiritual connection – seems to affect and influence the functioning of the physical heart and is central to our overall well-being. In *The Flame of the Heart*, author Torkom Saraydarian says that in the "Ageless Wisdom" this mysterious yet all important heart "refers to a golden twelve-petaled lotus located behind the physical heart about four to six inches away from the body," and that it distributes the energies of love, compassion and intuition and "links all beings and life forms in the world." (pp. 11-12) This also coincides with the more commonly referred to heart chakra, which is said to exist in the etheric body that surrounds our physical body and holds the electrogmagnetic and energetic patterns which affect and are affected by our physical, emotional and mental states.

Yet, despite the importance of this "greater" heart that serves as a feeling-wisdom bridge between soul and body, it is often held at the greatest distance from our choices and our life paths and purposes. It is very typical of humanity, drawn as we are to things outside of us, that we overlook the power and potency of what is right here, with and within us. The great paradox of the emotional heart is that while it is, conceptually, the softest, most vulnerable and easily hurt part of us, it is also our greatest strength and wisdom-source because it is our portal to the infinite resources of the Divine.

As Jay Ramsay says in *Alchemy - The Art of Transformation,* "Your heart is the wound and your heart is the key." (p. 130) There is probably no pain so unbearable as that of the disappointed, grief-stricken or broken heart. And yet, while here in the heart is our woundedness, also here in the heart, where the Angels amplify Divine Presence and Energy, is our greatest potential for transformation and rebirth. Shutting down our hearts – the most potent "fountain of youth" and rejuvenator available to us – is akin to shutting out life and life-giving energies both outgoing and incoming. Like a picked flower, without full access to the root of our emotional-intuitive heart's mysteries and meanings, we are cut off from the channel providing us Source-nutrients, and over time our potency and juiciness wane. Thus, when our heart is hurting, weakened or shut down, we need healing that is no less than transformational.

## ***Our Angelic Soulmates***

The 72 Angels in their heart-dominion work to not only help us heal and transform the effects that our hurts have had upon us, but also they help us to "true-up" ourselves at every level by showing us how to live a heart-driven life – which we are more and more able to do as our hearts are healed. We must offer up, like a prayer, the softer side of our will, which is *willingness*, and allow the Angels to bring light and lightness to what has been hidden, heavy, dark and despairing. With our permission, the Angels will begin to soften what is hard and crusted over. They will share our burden so that the weight is carried by shoulders *and* wings until we are healed. And they will bring a balm of peace – even before the effects of healing are apparent – to ease us in the moment. We will come to know, *through our willingness to feel*, that we are not facing anything in our lives – past, present or future – alone..

As the Angelic Energies show us what particularities of our inner Divinity we are here to embody and express, they amplify within us the Divine Qualities that they themselves embody which correspond to our own. By energetically dwelling within us, they magnify the holographic imprint of the Divine carried by our souls and reconnect us to our true identity and indwelling Divine "power-source." This is how the ancient mysteries of "As Above, So Below" or "on Earth as it is in Heaven" are accomplished and how our image and likeness to the Divine is quickened: by the Angelic Presences which dwell within our humanity as vibratory expressions, radiances or *angles* of Divine Light, illuminating and quickening the soul-magnitude of our own unique beingness within our hearts unto all the rest of our parts.

**"Bottled light.**" We need more light in our everyday life. If light could be bottled...well, the Angels would say that it is and we can partake at any time because we each are a living vessel of light! Granted, sometimes we are seeing "through the glass darkly," and others are looking at us through their glass darkly. But, as the Angels continually illuminate for us, the light we are looking for is within us.

In working with the Angels to expand the presence of love, which expands the greater truth of who we are, we can magnify and emanate as much light as we want and need. And we can take our awareness and interactions with the Angels into our daily lives by using their qualities and the messages in the Daily Wisdoms to transform how we interact with others and the events of our day. This can be as simple as welcoming every encounter and conversation with a smile – especially the difficult ones. And offering a helping hand, a comforting shoulder or depthful listening, even when someone lashes out. It is in our power to change what comes at us from the outer world by meeting it with something more loving from within us. Like "*the tail wagging the dog,*" often our reactions are simply the acting out from some previous harbored hurt. But if we "*lead from our heart, rather than our hurt,*" we – and the other – can be saved from our hurt by love.

And so, in the Daily Wisdoms, each Angel speaks to us from its heart-plane of influence and support, where it amplifies within us its particular qualities through the lens of Divine Love. Again, in the spirit of the Kabbalah as "the receiving," we are invited to draw inward to the altar of our hearts and receive the loving energetic support of our indwelling Angels. Here by our Divine-Human commingled light, we may cultivate love and compassion for self and others, sharpen the ability to hear our own soul-voice through intuition and heart-truth, and live by the wisdom that love cultivates from the knowledge and experience that we bring unto our hearts.

## ***Our personal "Birth Angels"***

The ancient wisdoms reveal that our souls come to Earth for many lifetimes in order to heal the unhealed hurts and issues that occur in human life, which Eastern traditions call our "karma." Thus may we advance the "dharma" of our soul purposes in service to the expansion of the Divine within ourselves and others. Because of the density and forgetfulness of Earth-life, it is said that in our soul-choice of circumstances for each lifetime we also choose certain influences, guides and cosmic aspects around our time of birth that will act as symbols and "signatures" to remind and help support us with what we came here to do.

**The concept of "signatures.**" I have been drawn over the last year to the writings of 16th century Christian mystic and theologian Jacob Boehme, who expanded upon the Doctrine of Signatures developed by Paracelsus (1491-1541) to determine the medicinal purposes of herbs and plants based on their forms and attributes. Boehme's work applied this doctrine spiritually as evidence of the God within us. He was banished by local ecclesiastics for, among other views, his heretical notions of an "inner Divine" whose Presence and Qualities are visible in the signatures of form and function in all living beings and things.

I venture to say that our innermost longing as human beings, in addition to the need for love and belonging, is to know who we are and what we are here for. Delving into the law of signatures from a spiritual perspective has helped me to understand the 72 Angels, and especially our Birth Angels, as signatures, i.e., clues, to our particular attributes, potentials and purposes in this life. Thus, the signatures of our Birth Angels are the correspondence of their dates of governing which correspond to our own birth date and time, as well as their qualities which support our own qualities, potentials and/or challenges. Additional signatures would be their astrological associations, their position on the Tree of Life, their overlighting Archangel, and more. While the qualities and functions of all 72 Angels encompass the vast spectrum of possibilities and purposes within us, our personal Birth Angels more particularly signify what we are here to do, heal, express and manifest in our current lifetime.

**The astrology connection.** Humankind has always sought clues to our meaning and purpose through the wonders of the natural world because of an intrinsic sense of the energies that inhabit and weave together all of life. The ancients regarded the patterns of the stars not only as Divine omens, but as energetic clues for decoding the patterns of light carried in our Divine souls and in the desires, purposes and potentials expressed through our human personalities. Discerning that the Divine-Human mysteries are encoded in the natural world and in all of Creation through number, quality and patterning, the wise men of the past studied the constellations of stars and other heavenly bodies, and all of nature's forms and ways, as a serious spiritual science. It was only when the medieval Christian church declared the study of the stars and Earth rites to be heretical in order to establish absolute authority and power for the church, that these were relegated to "occult," "pagan" and even "demonic" practices.

Medieval Kabbalists associated the 72 Angels with the particularities of our lives through their hierarchies of relationship to Creation and time. They understood that just as each of us represent a micro-expression of the galaxy that is our macrocosm (symbolized by the Zodiac), a kind of hologram of the Divine Totality is conveyed within us by all 72 Angels so that we may partake of that Totality as we ascend in consciousness.

In addition, just as we are born under certain cosmic aspects of sun, moon, stars and planets, we are also attended by a particular "constellation" of Angelic Energies who dwell with and within us and whose qualities of Divine Love-and-Truthness correspond to our unique soul purposes, challenges and potentials for this lifetime. Thus, the three Angels who were the supporting energies at the moment we were born work within us throughout our lives to help quicken and amplify the spark of Divinity that is our soul and its expression in time, meaning and matter.

It is important to distinguish that astronomical objects are creations, whereas the Angelic Energies are understood to be emanations of the Divine Itself. That said, nothing of either astrology or the Angelic realms is meant to govern or supplant our own will, but rather to increase our awareness of potential and lend energetic support to our own choices.

**Degrees/days**. Medieval Kabbalists working with the 72 Angels corresponded their hierarchies of governing to 360 degrees of the Zodiac, with each degree ideally correspondent to one day. However, we live in a 365-day solar year. From my research of ancient calendars, it seems that many early civilizations adhered to a lunar calendar of approximately 30 days per month x 12 months = 360 days. However, Earth's orbit around the sun is elliptical – not a perfect circle – and thus every few years certain civilizations would tack on an extra month to make up the difference between lunar and solar cycles. In 45 B.C., the Julian solar calendar was established, which took us to a 365.25-day year, with a "leap" year every four years. This was reformed by the slightly more accurate Gregorian calendar in 1582. Isaac Newton surmised in 1728 that the original 360-degree Zodiac was attributed to the early widespread use of a 360-day calendar. In order to reconcile degrees with days in working with the 72 Angels, some overlapping of dates had to occur to cover all 365/366 days. In my work, I refer to the correspondences of days rather than degrees because they are more universally relatable.

We can know our Birth Angels by corresponding our day and time of birth to the Angels' days and times of influence. (See the dates listed with the Daily Wisdoms and Appendix I, or *The 72 Angels* quick-reference chart at 72BirthAngels.com.) Note that because of the inexact correspondence between 360 degrees and 365+ days, if your day and time of birth are close to the "cusp" of the Angelic Energy before or after one of your Birth Angels, you may feel a resonance to work with that Angel as well.

Your Birth Angels interact with the physical, emotional and mental aspects of your being:

Your **Incarnation Angel** ~ Expresses qualities of the Divine Being and Will through human physical existence, will and life purpose. Corresponds to your five-day period of birth and supports the qualities, challenges and expressions of your physical being and the will to carry out your soul purposes in your human lifetime. Some like to refer to this Angel as our "Guardian Angel."

Your **Heart Angel** ~ Expresses qualities of Divine Love through the feelings and wisdoms of the human heart. Corresponds to your actual day of birth, your emotional qualities, challenges and potentials, and supports the cultivation of love, compassion, forgiveness and understanding for self and others, as well as intuition, wisdom and personal truth.

Your **Intellect Angel** ~ Expresses qualities of Divine Mind through the constructs and creations of human intelligence. Corresponds to your time of birth (within 20 minutes), your mental qualities, challenges and potentials and the cultivation of greater awareness and higher-mind. Those born at a cusp time (on the hour or 20 minutes before or after) may be said to have two Intellect Angels (for a total of four Birth Angels).

**Angel dynamics within us**. I would like to clarify the use of the term "govern." The Angels are spoken of as governing certain days and times, as well as the different planes of human beingness (physical, emotional and mental). What is meant by the term governing here is *influence*, *correspondence* and *support*. Ideally, because of our Divinely-endowed birthright of free will, we humans govern ourselves (an arguable concept!). The Angels, therefore, are not within and among us to govern us, but to bring a positive influence of Divine energies and support for our highest good – which is to amplify and magnify the truth of who we each are and support the fruition of our soul purposes and potentials in time and eternity.

# Life with the 72 Angels

The 72 Angels' Daily Wisdoms are given to help increase awareness and utilization of our magnificent inner resources – the soul-voice within our hearts and our Angelic support system designed to amplify the Divine within all the aspects of our human beingness, and to help us love and heal ourselves so that we might become all we came here to be. As we begin to experience the Angels in this new light, we see ourselves, each other and all of life in a greater light.

There is so much more to see than we are looking at, so much more to feel than we are reaching for, so much more to know than what has been handed down to us by others. And as we allow the Angels to take up more of our inner room, there is less space for doubts, fears, guilt, shame and old hurts and more room for the truth of who we are and the self-love that enables us to truly love others. Looking through our "Angel-eyes," we see the gifts waiting in the wings of every moment. In coincidental encounters and conversations we hear their uncanny and timely messages, and suddenly our daily lives become full of signs, wonders, symbols and clues to unlock the meanings and purposes of our gifts, opportunities and challenges.

## *Welcoming the Angels*

Through the Angels we come to understand that we each exist as a uniqueness of being and possibility within the Divine Oneness, and the Divine Oneness exists within us in order to experience life as only each of us can live it. Thus, when we welcome the Divine as the Angels, it is not that we ask them to come to us from "above" or "out there." What we are actually doing is inviting our own awareness to see and feel that they are already here within and around and among us. By welcoming them, we acknowledge their presence and our willingness to engage. Physical life is sort of like having been given a house with somebody already living in it who was so much a part of the woodwork that we didn't even notice them. Then one day we're bouncing off our own inner walls, and suddenly we sense – someone "else" is here! This is where willingness and receptivity are called into play so that we might enter into conversation and communion with that "hidden" magnificence within us, and let it shine!

And so, as in the Divine-Human mysteries of many spiritual paths, we are called to three things in our work and play with the Angels: **ask**, **receive** and **become**. This ongoing 3-step "Angel-alchemy" can transform our base *mettle* into the spiritual gold (light) of manifested love, truth, wisdom and a life fulfilled:

1. **Ask** (Invoke) – Pray/chant/speak the Angel's name, open your heart and invite its presence to expand within you.

2. **Receive** (Imbibe) – Breathe in, listen, meditate upon and allow the Angel's essence and energy to expand within your heart and being.

3. **Become** (Embody) – Absorb, digest and assimilate the Angel's qualities into the very belly of your beingness so that your awareness and your action come into harmony (as in "walking the talk").

These steps can be part of a meditation with the day's Angel and used to focus attention and awareness for everything you encounter during your day. Most importantly, follow the inner prompts from that not so still, not so small voice in your heart, for it may be the voice of the Angel within, in unison with your own soul. Slowly, even epiphanously, the effects become cumulative and life-transforming.

## ***The Alchemy of Angelic Awareness***

The Kabbalah tradition around the 72 Angels is deep and complex – but be assured that it's not necessary to understand most of what I've given you here in order to experience the energies and wisdoms of the Angels in deep and transformative ways. My own ongoing experience in co-creating the *Book of Days* with the Angels has been deeply transformative as emotional and mental sludge, moods and attitudes have been moved out of me in order to provide a more clear pathway for the Wisdoms to emerge. And it's not that I had to struggle with doing a particular ritual, but rather that I had to be willing to be present and patient with myself while the Angels were doing their work within and around me. The miracles of spiritual grace that occur in the heart are all about willingness.

As soon as you open yourself to the Angels with your awareness, they begin to work within you. Things start to happen in your life naturally because emotional and mental rocks of resistance have been rolled away from the cavern of your heart. Although grace is probably most often referenced to Christianity and the "Christ" that is the embodiment and expression of Divine Love, grace precedes and is not exclusive to any religion, nor can anyone prescribe how it will work with you.

Your grace-path is deeply personal and of utmost relevance to you and every iota of longing and circumstance in your life and being. But perhaps there is this common aspect, as the Angel ALADIAH says, "*Grace does not happen yesterday or tomorrow – it is a present that is given only in the present, in a moment of Presence.*" Whatever name or "affiliation" grace may ever go by, it is about the energy of a commingled Love and Truth which meets you in your heart, in whatever path, creed (or not), culture, vocabulary or circumstance – to birth the Light within you. When grace happens with the Angels, you embark upon a co-creative journey that enables you to become more fully and wholly human than you ever dared to imagine.

So, my suggestion is to make some quiet time for a few moments every day to read and contemplate the day's Angel-wisdom. Remember that the message is meant to speak to your heart, and note the parts that resonate with you. As you go through your day notice what is echoed in conversations and encounters, and where you can use the qualities of that day's Angel to approach yourself and others more heartfully. Pay attention to the moments that resonate and trigger a feeling, which will indicate a timely relevance to you. Begin to see the connections between you and everything and everyone which are sometimes signaled by coincidence and unexpected encounters.

For example, let's say the Angel of the day is ACHAIAH, who is all about patience. You may find that on ACHAIAH's day of support a lot of obstacles and slow people cross your hurried path to give you the opportunity to practice patience. After your initial resistance, a realization may begin to stir about what really matters and how nice it is to slow down a little and notice a bit of beauty around you that rushing would have missed – or to take a moment to give or receive a kindness that makes someone's day, even your own.

You may even want to keep a daily Angel journal of signs, happenings, coincidences, intuitions, feelings and thoughts. And if something unusual or interesting occurs, or perhaps you have an important meeting, you may also want to check the Intellect Angel governing at that very moment to prompt your awareness and inner support. Since the five volumes of Daily Wisdoms each deal with a particular aspect of our lives, you might want to read the Wisdom for the Angel from the volume that would relate to your issue or event. For example, if you have an argument or difficult encounter with your partner or family member, consult Volume 4, which deals with "Relationship with Others," and read the Wisdom for the Angel that was governing during the time period of your encounter. (See Appendix I for a list of corresponding times.)

## ***The Seasons of Our Lives***

As the Angels' daily messages were emerging, I could see that they were wanting to follow the flow and energies of the seasons as expressed not only in the natural world but also in our own lives. Just as with the Divine and the entire cosmos since the first moments of Emanation and Creation, everything and everyone is birthed, lives and moves forward through the cycles of life in the context of relationship. Thus, in the first cycle of 72 messages starting March 21, there is a focus on what the soul regards as our primary relationship, which is with the Divine Itself. Subsequent cycles throughout the year grow out of our relationship with the Divine into relationship with the self, our life meaning and purpose, important others in our immediate circles, and the world at large. Thus, these are the five seasons in the Angelic year:

**Spring** ~ 3/21–6/2: Relationship with the Divine. The newborn green of Spring symbolizes our cosmic birth and what the soul regards as our primary relationship with the Divine Itself as our origin. Just as with the Spring rebirth of many forms of Creation in the natural world, we too experience the quickening and joy of new beingness and awakening to the world in fresh ways as we sprout new beginnings and creations that have been gestating within us during the Winter.

**Summer** ~ 6/3–8/16: Relationship with Self. This is a time of exploration and celebration of ourselves through self-love, gladness, the lighterness of being, living, loving and playing in the present and the flowering and ripening of our unique potentials.

**Fall** ~ 8/17–10/29: Relationship with Work and Purpose. This is the season for harvesting the fruits of our summer and scattering new seeds as we get back to work after vacations and times of fun and relaxation. While outer forms begin to fall away, we begin a deeper exploration into meaning and purpose as we continue to cultivate our individuation through new ideas, projects and collaborations.

**The "Holy-days" of Late Fall/Early Winter** ~ 10/30–1/8: Relationship with Others. Here the Angels bring us to heart-and-mindfulness in our interpersonal relatings at the time of year when we gather with loved ones and those in our immediate circles to celebrate the holidays and holy days of the season. In coming together with those who matter most, where the need for forgiveness and healing is often most apparent, we see the opportunity through self-transformation to transform and enliven our relationships.

**Winter** ~ 1/9–3/20: Relationship with community and the world. In this last volume, the 72 Angels bring the five Angelic cycles of the year to completion. Here the Wisdoms address how we each bring our unique self, individuation, purposes and interpersonal relatings to our communities and the collective consciousness of the world, including the Earth. From the gestation and nurturing of our own withins during the dormancy of winter's inwardness, new ideas, wisdoms and ways soon begin to sprout for a renewed and even reborn self that we may bring to the awakening world.

**Angels for all seasons**. In acknowledgment to those who live in the southern hemisphere – Australia, New Zealand, South America, South Africa and so on – of course you experience the progression of the seasons in reverse of the northern hemisphre (loosely, Spring=Fall, Summer=Winter). Those who live closer to the equator in either hemisphere experience less dramatic differences in the seasons, except perhaps for seasonal water and wind events. Since the Divine meets us wherever we are, and I am in the northern hemisphere, the messages are given in this context. So while the seasonal correspondences in the Angel wisdoms may be similar to the emotional and circumstantial seasons of your life – the dates will be different for you.

Because we humans often have a hard time with change, it is helpful to remember that it is change that moves us forward. The well-known Buddhist phrase, "this too shall pass," not only speaks of the changing seasons of our lives, but also the cycles of waxing, fullness and waning within each season – much like the cycles of day to night in the 24-hour day, the monthly moon cycles, or the changing of our moods from one minute to the next! So flows each of the five cycles with the 72 Angels. Thus, in each cycle the first Angel, VEHUIAH, is all about beginnings, and the Angels that follow support the qualities and capacities that are needed to make a good beginning and move toward growth, flowering, ripening, fruition, harvest, and then the waning that ends with the 72$^{nd}$ Angel MUMIAH, which supports endings in preparation for rebirth. So then we start again with the next cycle – but now we're in a different season, which brings different atmospheres, colors, opportunities and experiences to another cycle of the Angels and the dynamics of our lives. It's like a grand circle dance between the same and different spiraling throughout time! Perhaps a little like getting up with the same person (even oneself) for 50 years and realizing every day there is still something new to discover.

Through the Angelic energies I have come to better understand the spiritual dynamics in the déjà vu of lessons we thought we had already learned. Although a scenario may seem like an old one, what is new and different now is us – and thus we are being given an opportunity to heal any residue of that past by making a different choice in this new present. At the same time, there is perhaps also being offered a chance to work at a deeper level to heal some last little bit which we are now ready for.

Our cosmic constant is our soul existence; however while in physical life we are a constant that is always changing – which progresses our soul through time in cycles within cycles: from our cosmic birth as a soul to the incarnations of our soul in a multitude of lives, to the cycles within each life, and the seasons within each of those cycles. Ultimately, the deeper potential in all our life cycles is not the material goods, stature or wealth we amass with our clever minds and machinations, but what we feel and experience with our hearts, which not only survives life and death, but accumulates beyond time into eternity.

## *Going with the Angelic Flow of Spring*

Spring is the time of year when all that has been hidden and secretly gestating in the natural world comes to light. Everywhere the newborn green cotyledons of early growth are breaking the surface of the soil straining toward the light and warmth that, along with the rain, will eventually bring them into flowering and fruition. If you live in a four-season part of the world, it is such a gift to see the bright green lushness after the bareness of Winter which, except for the evergreens, seemed to belie any life at all! The Earth has resiliently withstood its own silent, cold, dark and barren landscapes, and is now bursting back to life. Birdsong is bringing in an earlier dawn, while all the creatures that live their lives in a universe of dirt, grasses, stones and trees are coming alive and making nests for new babies – for of course, Spring is the season of birthing for many creatures, including humans.

The ancients understood that the new enlivening we experience in Spring is a reflection and re-enactment of the birth of Creation and our own cosmic birth, the quickening of soul within our body, and the burgeoning of potential in every part of our being. Peoples like the Celts and Druids, as well as indigenous cultures and seemingly pantheistic traditions, would "worship" nature and her seasons and cycles as facets, forces and qualities of the Divine Presence inhabiting and expressing Itself on Earth and in the humus of humanity. While "civilized" cultures were building churches and temples out of wood and stone where they could visit and hear God once or twice a week, people who they called "pagans" would live and commune with God every day in the natural world, honoring the diversity of the Divine within every living thing and being.

However disconnected from the rhythms of the Earth as we "moderns" may have become, still for many of us there is no season that re-enlivens us the way Spring does. Often we too have been deep within our own inner humus during the dormancy and darkness of winter, reassessing our direction, weighing meaning and purpose in work and relationships or conceiving new ideas, imaginings and beginnings. And then suddenly – the "let there be light" of Spring puts a quickening in our hearts and our steps. New ideas that were simmering now have a fire in them, and we see our potentials and possibilities as beginning actualities in a literal new light. And underlying all of this is Spring's expression of our utmost hope – the joy of seeing and feeling that life truly does go on, no matter how dark and barren it may ever seem. Indeed, Life itself wants to live – and we are here so that it can live through us!

# The Daily Wisdoms

*The 72 Angels' Days of Heart Influence*

---

As the first *Birth Angels* book goes into with more detail, each Angel has a variety of associations related to the its position on the Tree of Life, which also give clues to its nature: the Sephira of the Tree in which the Angel resides, its overlighting Archangel, astrological and date associations and more.

**Sephirot Pages**: These introduce the Sephira (vessel or sphere) in which each group (choir) of eight Angels reside in nine of the Ten Sephirot of the Tree of Life, as well as the qualities and functions of the overlighting Archangel.

**Date**: The current day of the Angel's expression and support through our heart plane is bolded; the other dates represent its four other "heart-days" of influence and support during the year. Since it is helpful to be aware of your Heart Angel not only on your birthday, but also its other four days of influence, you may want to mark your personal calendar with all five days. Note also that the yearly cycle for the 72 Angels begins March 21, the time of the Spring Equinox, which is the beginning of "Nissan," the first month of the year in the Jewish calendar. In my research I also ran across an obscure variant in the date attributions of the Angelic cycles, but the one used in all the *Birth Angels* materials is the cycle that the $12^{th}$-$15^{th}$ century school of Isaac the Blind and his followers and fellow Kabbalists were working with throughout the centuries. (See Appendix II for more info.)

An Angel's full day of influence goes from 12:00 am midnight to 12:00 am midnight, 24 hours later (00:00-24:00 in Europe, etc.). A few of the Angels' days overlap to support a total of 365 days. In a leap year of 366 days, the Angel for February 28 also governs the $29^{th}$. The "am" designation always goes from 12:00 am midnight to 12:00 pm noon (00:00-12), and the "pm" from 12:00 pm noon to

12:00 am midnight (12:00-24:00). Of course, 12:00 is a cusp minute for both day and night. An Angel that governs for a day and a half, for example, 4/16 + 17 am, would span from 12:00 am midnight as the 15th passes to the 16th, to 12:00 pm noon on the 17th (midnight to midnight to noon) (00:00-24:00-12:00).

Note: Kabbalists have historically worked with the 72 Angels through their correspondences to the Zodiacal degrees totaling 360, the circumference of a circle. Ultimately a correspondence of degrees to actual days was needed in order to accommodate our 365-day calendar, which meant that a few of the Angelic Energies would be attributed to more than one day. Because the degrees to days correspondences change slightly every year, it can be helpful to be aware of the Angelic Energy that comes before and after each of your Birth Angels or the one you are working with at a particular date or time, and notice if you feel more resonance with one more than another. (Thanks to Tristan Llop, son of Kabaleb, for explaining this to me!) Ultimately our lives are about what we do with the energies that present themselves to us – for we have the innate power to use everything that comes our way as an ally.

**The Angel's number and name**: The number for each Angel represents the order of its position on the Tree of Life and its degrees of correspondence to the Zodiacal wheel of time – and if you study astrology and numerology these may give additional insight into both the Angels and the stars. The Angel's name is a transliteration of its Hebrew name. The origin of the names is from what the Kabbalah refers to as the 72 "Intelligences" or "Names of God" as the "Shem HaMephorash,"), which are each composed of a three-letter combination derived from a "decoding" of Exodus 14:19-21 in Hebrew. While vowels were originally left out of the Angels' Hebrew Names to create ambiguity in order to protect the sacred Names of God, in later centuries the "niqqud" (vowel marks) were added to help with pronunciation. Each Angel's name ends in either "IAH" or "EL," denoting that the name is a Name and Quality of God. I have found in some Kabbalah literature that IAH represents the feminine aspect and EL the masculine, representing the inherent masculine-feminine unity within the Divine which is expressed in duality as polarities, as with all manifestations in life.

You will notice if you consult other sources through the ages that the spellings of the Angels' names vary greatly. This is the result of varied dialects and permutations in the Hebrew language and its transliterations through centuries of dispersion of the Jewish people into different cultures and sects. I have done extensive research on this, but in the end have chosen to follow most of the spellings that the works of Kabaleb put forth based on his extensive research of prominent medieval and Renaissance Kabbalists working with this system. (See Appendix II herein for details.)

**Pronunciation guide**: This is given to help with saying or chanting the Angel's name aloud in meditation or prayer as you invite the Angel's energies to expand within you. All the names are emphasized (shown in ALL CAPS) on the last syllable, IAH or EL, to show that the name is a quality and aspect of God. Names with more than two syllables have two accented syllables, as in "Neh-MA-mee-YAH." Kabbalah creation cosmology regards the sounds and forms of the Hebrew letters as having the power to transmit Divine Energies and even bring forth new life. This is akin to the use of the word "Om" and Sanskrit chants to invoke the Divine within.

**Angel's quality/function and G/R/S designation**: This represents the Divine attribute which the Angel embodies and amplifies within you, and whether the attribute is expressed outwardly (G, for "Going out" from the Divine and down the Tree of Life toward manifestation), inwardly (R for "Returning" back up the Tree to the Divine through ascending consciousness), or in a state of equilibrium which can be expressed outwardly or inwardly (S for Stabilized).

As discussed in the section "Our Personal Birth Angels," the qualities of the Angels seem to have been attributed beyond the literal meanings of their Hebrew letters to reflect in part their astrological associations according to medieval astrologers working within the Kabbalah and the 72 Angels tradition.

**Keynote phrase**: This is a short by-line I have added to capture the essence of the Angel's function.

**Overlighting Archangel**: This is the Archangel that governs the Sephira which the Angel resides within on the Tree of Life, and whose qualities overlight or influence the functions of the eight Angels in that Sephira and the Angelic order (choir) that the Angels belong to. There are eight Angels in each of the Nine (out of Ten) Sephirot on the Tree (8x9=72). Because so many people working with Angels in our modern world seem to be working with the Archangel energies, it is perhaps interesting to note that throughout the world's Angelic traditions and the ancient wisdoms, Archangels' were seen as the guardians of lands, nations and societal groups; whereas the Angels are said to be attendant to individuals because their vibrations are nearer to life forms. However, until this tradition was revealed in the 1980's-90's by the work of Kabaleb (first published under his friend Haziel's name), only a few of the Angels' individual names have been commonly known to modern angelology.

**The Angel's sign, planet and 5-day period of "Incarnation" influence**: The Angel's astrological correspondences relate to its five consecutive days of influence once a year on the Incarnation, or physical, plane, which also corresponds to 5 degrees of the Zodiac (72x5=360) – taking into consideration the adjustments made for a 365-day year (see Appendix I). If you are interested in astrology, this can help to shed additional light on the Angel's qualities. (Neptune and Uranus were added later when they were discovered.) Although the Angels in their Incarnation influence (physicality, will and life purpose) are not the focus of the *Book of Days*, I added the dates of each Angel's Incarnation influence (the date spread next to the sign/planet) for ease in discovering your Incarnation Angel – which would be the one supporting the five-day span that corresponds to the five-days around your birth. For example, if your birthday is March 18, your Incarnation Angel would be #72 MUMIAH, which governs March 16-20. However, because of the yearly fluctuation of degrees correspondent to days, if your birthday is the first or last day or the Angel's date-span of support, then it is suggested to pay attention to the Angel closest to yours, being the previous or next, whichever applies – and notice which is more resonant. (See also Appendix I for a complete list of the 72 Angels with their corresponding 5-day span of Incarnation influence, as well as the 20-minute period during the 24-hour day when they support our intellect.)

**"I AM THAT WHICH...:"** Here the Angel introduces itself as a particularized aspect ("that which") of the One "I AM" which is its purpose to amplify in our human lives – thus helping us to fulfill the unique "I Am That Which" that each of us are as a particular constellation and expression of Divine-Human qualities.

**The Angel's message**: As detailed above, all 72 Angels cycle for at least one day five times a year, effectively taking us through the seasons of the year and of our lives. Since everything and everyone exists in the context of relationship, the first cycle of 72 messages starting March 21 starts with the new birth of the natural world which also symbolizes the soul's cosmic birth and relationship to the Divine. From there we move into the four subsequent cycles – our relationship with self, our work and purposes, others in our close circles, and then to our communities and the world at large. Thus, all five cycles comprise a journey in one year through all the literal and symbolic themes and seasons of our lives.

You may notice that the Angels have different tones in their "speech" at different times – some are lighter, some more serious, some "teacherly" and others passionate. Also, sometimes they speak as "I" and sometimes as "we." I continue to sense that in their roles as differentiated expressions of the Divine Oneness, "I" and "we" are interchangeable for them. The messages of course come through my own within and are mingled with the vocabularies and meanings which I am able to discern – and the more I bring myself into their presence with love, the more and better I am able to hear. The light-thread that is woven through all the different messages is about the power of love to reveal and expand the truth of who we are and what we are here to be and do for ourselves, each other and the Divine Itself.

**The "Amen" at the end of each Wisdom.** I realized I had been hearing "Amen" at the end of each Wisdom from the beginning of the *Book of Days* and had not been fully conscious of it until working on the third volume! "Amen" is a word of power in Hebrew, a kind of cosmic "abracadabra" to activate the Divine in human life. In researching the word's origins, there were the usual Hebrew and Christian uses of Amen as "so be it" at the end of prayers, as well as other correspondences: Amen encompasses the Hebrew letters "aleph-mem-nun" (confirmed, reliable, have faith, believe), which also correspond to the word "emuna" (faith) and "emet" (truth). There are also associations with the Egyptian god Amun (also Amen, the creator of all things, king of the gods) and the Hindu Sanskrit word Aum (or Om, the Absolute, Omnipresent, Manifest and Unmanifest). In suddenly becoming fully aware of the "Amen" that was naturally emerging at the end of each wisdom, I realized that the intent of the Angelic Energy was that the words would not only inspire but also *transmit* the energies of their meaning unto those "who have the heart to hear." In the cacophony of life and its demands, we may have the heart to hear in one moment and not in another – so the word Amen is a word to call us back to our hearts from wherever else we are. And so here, as "Amen...," the three dots are meant to extend a loving and compassionate space to do that.

Remember, again, that the Daily Wisdoms are given as messages from the 72 Angels when they are in their "heart dominion," to amplify qualities of Divine Love to support our cultivation of self-love and love of others, as well the other resources of the heart which are compassion, understanding, forgiveness, intuition, soul-truth and wisdom. As the Angel JELIEL conveys in Volume 1,

> *The Love we bring is a Love composed of as many different qualities, forms, faces and expressions as there are*

*people...a Love that contains all purposes and possibilities...a Love that will be your anchor against time's fickle winds of change and the sometimes stormy seas of life. A Love-light of Truth by which you may see finally that however long or far you seek, what you are looking for is always right here in your heart of hearts, prompting you to ask, beckoning you to receive, inviting you to shine forth more and more of who you truly are. And to know once and for all that, truly, you are not alone – for there is always someone at home...within.*

And so now, may you embark upon your daily heart-journey with the 72 Angels, the joy of the season's inward bounty and the nurturing of new seeds in your heart, mind, body and soul!

# March 21 – 28

---

## Angels 1 – 8

---

*Sephira 1*

### KETHER ~ Crown/Will

*Overlighting Archangel*

**METATRON ~ "Angel of the Presence"**
Enlightenment, the connection of Light between
God's energy and human spiritual energy
(Related to the prophet Enoch & Akashic Records)

---

**1 VEHUIAH**
**2 JELIEL**
**3 SITAEL**
**4 ELEMIAH**
**5 MAHASIAH**
**6 LELAHEL**
**7 ACHAIAH**
**8 CAHETEL**

**3/21** * 6/3 * 8/17 * 10/30 * 1/9

# 1 VEHUIAH

(vay-HOO-ee-YAH)

***Will and New Beginnings*** (G)

*'One who begins again and again'*

Archangel ~ METATRON

Aries / Uranus (3/21-25)

---

I AM THAT WHICH...

*holds the 'light-template' of the first creation act by the Divine which is imprinted in every part of your beingness in order to spark the fires of initiative for you to enter new life cycles and forge new futures. On this and every new day of every new beginning, my light-stuff carried in your soul works within your heart and mind to help bring your ideas and imaginings into being, and through your body to replenish the energies of your physicality. As the ocean of feeling in your Divinely-human heart compels all your parts in collaboration, may you draw also from the light of the new sun to stoke the fire in your belly. Like the expanding breadth of trees drawing down the nutrients of light for the growth of new life, allow the branching out of your mind to be nourished by new information and experience. Let the winds of change blow away the wisps of yesterday so that you may breathe in the life-giving elixirs of all that is new and vibrant and on its way to you. For you are Divinely endowed with the power to do all these things and more!*

*And may you undertake all you desire with the initiative and magnificent determination of your own true will! For your will is born of the Divine Will that you live your unique and wonder-full life fully. As you go forth, also draw from the softer side of your will, which is willingness – not as a submission or abdication of your will – but in co-creation with your inner Divine that knows and loves your true soul-self in all its totality – including that of you which has not yet manifested in your Earth time and place.*

*I, VEHUIAH, who am given to accompany you at every 'starting gate' in your life, say this unto you: Even as we are the glorious varieties of hues and expressions of Divine Light and the boundless Love and Truth that is our collective nature, so are you as Divine Light-Seeds sprouted from the Divine Itself, formed inwardly in Its image and likeness to root the Heavens upon Earth. And so now, let your heart awaken as the Angelic rooted within you stirs, and your transformation begins. Amen...*

**3/22** * 6/4 * 8/18 + 19am * 10/31 * 1/10

# 2 JELIEL

(YAY-lee-EL)

***Love and Wisdom*** (G)

*'One who uses love to make wisdom'*

Archangel ~ METATRON

Aries / Saturn (3/26-30)

---

I AM THAT WHICH...

*illumines you and all your beginnings with the light of Universal Love so that you may come to know you are made of love and that it is love which gives meaning and motion to the truth of who you are and all you do. While you may relate to the concept of love as feeling, compassion, kindness and so forth – in its full nature, love is the energy of creation. Love, as the universal energy-in-motion which manifests, evolves and expands the truth of your own 'isness' – is the same Love which moved and continues to move the Truth of the Divine I AM to reveal and manifest the inherent diversity of Its Oneness into the diversity of Creation. Thus, to understand the great paradoxical gift of life is to realize that the diversities of humankind and all things and beings express and mirror the hidden diverse nature of God-the Oneness, so that the unique expression of truth that is carried within your soul might have time and space to expand and evolve. This is the ageless wisdom that love imparts: just as with the Divine Itself, love is how the truth of you is revealed and increased.*

*So powerful is the presence of love in your humanity, that while encased in the dense vibrations and challenges of Earth-life, the layers of forgetting, the pull of pleasure and pain, and your constant attraction to matter, you long to love and be loved and to draw upon love to manifest your dreams and purposes. In your heart of hearts you know that all you strive for on Earth and all the secrets of life worth seeking and finding are found in love. It is love that connects you with your fellow beings, and it is love that enables you to discern and implement your true soul-purposes on Earth. This is because you were loved into being from the Divine Itself, and thus you are made of the Love that expands the Truth of the Divine I AM through the unique expression of your own personal "I am" truth.*

*For those born to life in difficult or seemingly loveless circumstances, know in your highest aspirations and hopes that it is a greater Love which brought you forth and continues to sustain you. Draw on this Love to understand that your soul chose your human life conditions in order to accelerate your soul growth and human possibilities. The greater your challenges, the greater your potential and the sweeter your fulfillment. May you use the love within you, that is you, to continue to bring more and more of who you truly are into being, and in turn, love your own creations into being.*

*And know this always: Love does not want your humanity to get out of the way to bring something 'higher'-'better'-'greater' through you – Love wants you to* **become** *the way by claiming the greatness that is already born within you, waiting to be recognized and nourished. For love is the great alchemist of transformation, with the power to bring any part of you which has forgotten you are love into the remembering of your true nature. I, JELIEL, am the light within you given to illuminate the inner corridors of Love that hold all your parts together, and to help transform all your knowledge and experience into wisdom. For only Love can discern and invoke the whole truth of a thing, circumstance or being. Amen...*

**3/23** * 6/5 * 8/19pm + 20 * 11/1 * 1/11

# 3 SITAEL

(SIT-ah-EL)

***Construction of Worlds*** (G)

*'One who loves creations into being'*

Archangel ~ METATRON

Aries / Jupiter (3/31-4/4)

---

I AM THAT WHICH...

*represents the 'Master Builder,' the energy which conveys the designs of the Divine Architect unto all forms, including your own humanity and all your creations and works. All things and beings are composed of patterns that have the attributes of number and meaning, form and essence, quantity and quality, with humans being the most intricate on Earth. What you call 'sacred geometry' reveals the Divine patterns at play not only in the forms of nature such as snowflakes and flower petals, seeds and crystals, starfish and nautilus shells, stones and star constellations – but also in the delicate geometry and numerical aspects of the genetic codes and molecular, cellular and structural formations that compose all living beings. While these physical patterns compose the structures of all matter, both animate and inanimate, as well as signify and facilitate the functions of their components, they also mirror the light-code structures of essence and meaning in your soul-body. Together, these physical and essential patterns that construct the entirely of your being testify to the presence and purpose of the Divine and its infinite diversity of expression in Creation. Thereby is the light of Divine Love and Truth placed and purposed within your soul, heart, mind and body.*

*The physical integrity of life forms, or any kind of creation, is sustained, expanded and evolved by love. Thus, in each thing that you create, the secret to calling forth the Divine Essence and Power held within the patterns – even before they have been rendered into matter – is to love it. And by your love, the thing may become more than its form.*

*Just as you were loved into being, love what you desire to create, even before you know what it is – and your love will help it to find its true form and bring it and its meaning all the way into being. Thus is my light as SITAEL given unto you, that you may bring forth structures that reflect the integrity of truth-in-beingness. And as you draw from the mysteries of love to seek, find and manifest the essential truth of whatsoever you desire to create, it shall thereby be an expression of the truth of you as an expression of the Divine Itself. Amen...*

**3/24** * 6/6 * 8/21 * 11/2 * 1/12

# 4 ELEMIAH

(eh-LEM-ee-YAH)

***Divine Power*** (G)

*'One who implants the tree of life within'*

Archangel ~ METATRON

Aries / Mars (4/5-9)

---

I AM THAT WHICH...

*plants the light-seeds of Divinity within you so that the spiritual fruit of the Tree of Life may grow, ripen and flower as the fulfillment of your spiritual, emotional, mental and physical humanity. The ongoing power of creation is the greatest wonder in all the universes, and you carry this power within you as a legacy, a birthright and a natural expression of the Divine nature within your humanness. Like a fragile seedling that is a hybrid of two worlds, you are born with an unlimited potential to embody both the Divine and the Human for a magnificent, even 'super-charged,' life on Earth. For this you need nourishment and support not only from outer resources, but also your precious inner resources. Your world provides and cultivates the outer, while the spiritual realm cultivates your inner.*

*The natural world gives you light, warmth, air and water; but in order to fulfill your potential and purpose on Earth you must also draw from the well of your heart, which pumps its light-elixirs from your soul and its Divine lifeline to our eternal world in order to quench the thirst for meaning in yours.*

*Here in your heart, where I, the ELEMIAH light-power, dwell within you, you may draw through your own soul an unlimited supply of Divine Love, Creativity and Power to bring you, your relationships and everything about your human experience into a loving and true fullness of being. But because your humanity has been endowed with the power to choose, this is the question to answer at every deciding moment of your life: will you drink from this cup of Love for the truth and fullness of your life? Amen...*

**3/25** * 6/7 * 8/22 * 11/3 * 1/13

# 5 MAHASIAH

(ma-HA-see-YAH)

***Rectification*** (G)

*'One who returns to what is true for love's sake'*

Archangel ~ METATRON

Aries / Sun (4/10-14)

---

## I AM THAT WHICH...

*illuminates from within you the areas of your life which need 'course-correcting' and healing, and offers multitudes of second chances for the sincere-hearted! It is not about how many times you seem to fail, for failure exists only in the worlds of fear; but rather, it is about how willing you are, for love's sake, to persevere in that which is true for you. In the dynamics of Love and Truth, which compose the fabric of all life, every thing, being, relationship and event is an opportunity to engage with and expand the light which displaces all darkness inner and outer. Rectification is about the returning of things and beings to their natural state of harmony and ease without shame, guilt, regret, self-judgment, punishment or dogmatic rituals of atonement. For the true opportunity of healing is to come back into oneness with yourself and with the Divine who is your own inner light.*

*The process of rectification does not have to be a complex one, and there is no judge – only the 'inner discerner' that is your true and compassionate self. That said, we wish you to understand that the acquisition of knowledge cannot 'redeem' you, nor can all the good deeds in the world restore you to yourself – especially if you undertake these as some secret atonement for 'sins' against your true self or others. No matter what it may seem you have done or not done, the pilgrimage for true at-onement is simply the return journey to the altar of your heart, from wherever else you ever are, to claim the Love that is alive and desiring to breathe more and more of your soul into beingness at every moment.*

*Like life's natural movements of in and out and ebb and flow, your inner is always moving toward your outer for expression and experience, as your outer moves toward your inner for meaning and purpose. These are what move you through the healing seasons of your life, and I, MAHASIAH, am here within you to light the way out and the way in, again and again, with the love and compassion that is given freely and forever. Amen...*

**3/26** * 6/8 * 8/23 * 11/4 * 1/14

# 6 LELAHEL

(LAY-la-HEL)

***Light of Understanding*** (G)

*'One who transforms knowledge'*

Archangel ~ METATRON

Aries / Venus (4/15-20)

---

I AM THAT WHICH...

*awakens you to the Source of Creation whose light is ever-present within you so that you might see and understand who and why you are and continue to co-create yourself in that light. Knowledge by itself is like a husk without the grain, a fruit with no seeds, words with no content, beauty without depth. It is not enough to know something, for the way of Light is the assimilation of knowledge into a loving fullness of meaning. Knowledge can contribute to a greatness of mind; but for knowledge to be relevant and useful to your life, it must come into the presence of your heart and the love that deepens and ennobles everything you think you know. Here is where wisdom is made and understanding is born. Here, in your heart of hearts is where your soul reveals itself as a welling up of feeling that enables you to recognize the emerging truth of yourself – the what and why of your very beingness.*

*In the after-moments of the Divine 'Let there be Light,' what had been unseen and unknown became illuminated and the Divine beheld the infinite diversity of its own potential. Likewise, when you truly see yourself, you will understand that there is no end to what you are part and expressive of. And there is no end to what you may be and create through the greatness of that First Light of*

*Creation that is carried in your soul and which shimmers within you, through you and as you.*

*I, LELAHEL, am light-working here within your heart to help deepen the knowledge that you accumulate from the world into an understanding of the gift of your life. For only with understanding will you know what to do and be with what you know – and also how to live with what you don't yet know or understand without judging or dismissing its possibility. Dare to consider, even before you approach knowing anything or anyone, that all beings and things, all thoughts and ideas, feelings and 'facts,' exist within the greater reality of the Divine I AM through your own and everyone's unique isness. There is no one or no thing which is lesser – only different and unique expressions of that which is All. And above all your understandings may you understand this, deeply and truly: you are not 'only human.' You are a two-part-in-one Divine-Human being by virtue of the soul-spark of the Divine that animates your humanity. If you spend your life seeking to understand the scope of this, you will come to understand everything! So be it. Amen...*

**3/27** * 6/9 * 8/24 * 11/5 * 1/15

# 7 ACHAIAH

(a-KA-hee-YAH)

***Patience*** (G)

*'One who brings the stillness'*

Archangel ~ METATRON

Taurus / Mercury (4/21-25)

---

I AM THAT WHICH...

*helps you to experience the 'isness' that waits in the space between ebb and flow, between one word or musical note and another, between one heartbeat and the next, between breath in and breath out. Be here, in the in-between, and let stillness bring you to the bright star of the 'I Am' which shimmers within the heart of your being as the spark of light that is You as soul.*

*Worldly concerns are always about time – running out of it, wishing for more of it, rueing its passage, fearing its progression, and so on. In a stillness of presence, you come to realize that you have all the time and timelessness that you could ever need or want. And that in both time and the eternal all happenings and becomings, departures and arrivals occur in just the right moment for the bigger picture of your life-time – as well as for the soul of you which is not bound by beginnings and endings. When you push against time, you are resisting the natural flow, pushing the river of life, so to speak. Every thing and being, every happening in your life has its time. Slow down your hurrying so that you can feel and be in the flow of your life and let time unfold you. The bright star at your center will not let you be left behind or cast into darkness without an inner companion to light your extraordinary way.*

*I, ACHAIAH, am, and we all angelically are, your light-companions who 'fan' the eternal flame of Divinity within your humanness. Come within, into the stillness, and see by this light the 'I Am' that you are so uniquely an expression of – and in this moment....simply be and know that you are I AM. Amen...*

**3/28** * 6/10 * 8/25 * 11/6 * 1/16

# 8 CAHETEL

(KA-heh-TEL)

***Divine Blessings*** (G)

*'One who conducts the flow of plenty'*

Archangel ~ METATRON

Taurus / Moon (4/26-30)

---

I AM THAT WHICH...

*illuminates the blessings of the Divine inherent within you and always flowing toward you and all of life for the exuberance of creativity, nourishment and manifestation. Life is naturally blessed with possibility and plenty, for it is the nature of Life Itself to endow all form and essence with the means to multiply and thrive. Just as it is the inherent nature of the seed to blossom into that which it truly and fully is according to its species and uniqueness of variation, this is your birthright too. The difference between you and the seed is that you have the capacity to facilitate, focus and guide your own blossoming with your thinking mind and feeling heart.*

*The river of blessings continually flows, and it is up to you to choose your place in the river and to keep it clear and free of obstacles so that the flow might continue unimpeded. You can try to push the river or redirect it, but if you rather would learn its secrets and become part of the river itself, you will want for nothing. The evidence of this is in what the river has already brought you.*

*While you may think about blessings as the anticipation or hope for your next acquisition and tomorrow's bestowal of goods and good fortune, the blessings you already have are often overlooked. However, if ever your powers of acquisition are curbed for a time, use that time as an opportunity to realize your abundance of blessings in family and friendship, talents and abilities – and the things right in front of you and within you that with creativity can be repurposed and proliferated. In these times, you remember to 'count your blessings' and realize that those which are most significant are countless.*

*And so I, CAHETEL, invite you to consider the blessings in your life which are immeasurable. And while you are counting the uncountable, realize that your soul has the eternal 'on tap.' If you feel empty or lacking, it is because your 'pipeline' needs to drill deeper into your own within, pushing through fear and resistance, to where your true richness lies. Here, deep in your inner, you will learn how to be in the outer world – and how to have what truly belongs to your purpose and fulfillment in this lifetime. Thus, dear one, if you would siphon that eternal flow from within you, let the well of your heart spill over with gratitude until it becomes the ever-flowing river of your life. And know, ultimately, that there is no greater blessing you can give to another than the light-flow of your love and compassion. Amen...*

# March 29 – April 5

---

## Angels 9 – 16

---

*Sephira 2*

**CHOKMAH ~ Wisdom**

*Overlighting Archangel*

**RAZIEL ~ 'Secrets of God'**
Spiritual guidance, keeper of wisdom
and revealer of the mysteries

---

**9 HAZIEL**
**10 ALADIAH**
**11 LAUVIAH**
**12 HAHAIAH**
**13 YEZALEL**
**14 MEBAHEL**
**15 HARIEL**
**16 HAKAMIAH**

## **3/29** * 6/11 * 8/26 * 11/7 * 1/17

# 9 HAZIEL

(HA-zee-EL)

***Divine Mercy and Forgiveness*** (S)

*'One who sees with the light of love'*

Archangel ~ RAZIEL

Taurus / Uranus (5/1-5)

---

I AM THAT WHICH...

*conveys the unconditional love of the Divine for your humanity, and thus not only absolves, but precedes, all error that is ever perceived or judged against yourself or others. This beneficence is echoed in the most loving relationships of parents for children. You love them just because they are, and though you give them guidance and protection you ultimately help them to choose their own way because you love them. And when they seem to go astray and you and they may suffer for it, still you are merciful and forgiving because it is the nature of your great love to do so. And so it is with the Divine that parents you with both 'roots and wings' – you who are born from the Light and Love that shall never leave you, and yet set aloft with your own will and ways to create unique combinations of matter and meaning in a world that is waiting for what only you can be and give.*

*Your world is a great challenge, and because of your great courage to take it on, I, HAZIEL, and all the Angelic host are always attending you. Because of Love, you are always already forgiven –* ***because Love is for giving you back to yourself****. Because of the Light of Truth and Love's power to see the whole truth, mercy knows who you truly are. You must only open your heart and feel us within you, holding this lantern of Love and Truth* *that shall never dim and through which the true nature of you and all beings shall at last be illuminated. Receive this light unto yourself, and ever so gently and mercifully, do not hesitate to offer it unto each other, again and again. Amen...*

**3/30** * 6/12 + 13am * 8/27 * 11/8 * 1/18

# 10 ALADIAH

(a-LA-dee-YAH)

***Divine Grace*** (G)

*'One who endows you with the yes of life'*

Archangel ~ RAZIEL

Taurus / Saturn (5/6-10)

---

## I AM THAT WHICH...

*helps you to return to unity with and within yourself and the Oneness that is All, while bringing you the Love and Light which enable you to feel that you are felt, known and seen for the beauty of your unique self within the whole. I, ALADIAH, want you to know this: Grace does not happen yesterday or tomorrow – it is a present especially for you that is given only in the present, in a moment of Presence. To experience grace is to glimpse for a blissful eternal moment your foreverness shimmering in the gifts of life and time – and to feel the valuable sacredness of both your individuation and your oneness with all that is, seen and unseen. This is the paradox and potential of human life – to realize that on Earth you are an eternal being in a temporal setting. Embracing and rejoicing in this, rather than suffering from a sense of unbelonging, can set you free to be the everything you are as a being of two worlds.*

*You are both your inner and your outer, your matter and your meaning, your being and your becoming. If you desire to live on Earth in the grace of your true nature, then say yes to all of life, and be not caught up in the 'either/or' of life's seeming dualities. Say yes to what is and what comes, and then make your own path through, with or around it. Say yes to what goes, and be blessed by the gifts that every goodbye leaves you with. Say yes to the love that never leaves but only changes its form and face now and then to show you how to recognize it in everything and everyone. Say yes to who you are even while you are still bringing forth the more of you. Say yes to the shining other that is in front of you and beside you and inside you. Say yes. Feel yes. Be yes, full of grace. Amen...*

**3/31** * 6/13pm + 14 * 8/28 * 11/9 * 1/19

# 11 LAUVIAH

(LO-vee-YAH)

***Victory*** (G)

*'One who turns every moment into a win'*

Archangel ~ RAZIEL

Taurus / Jupiter (5/11-15)

---

I AM THAT WHICH...

*endows you with a great accumulation of light, knowledge and clarity to help you triumph in your everyday life by winning the battles that cannot be fought. It is the nature of Life Itself that you should flourish, be fulfilled and 'win at being you.' Worldly success may serve your soul growth at times, and at other times may not. When either success or seeming defeat seems to dim your inner light and take you farther into the forgetting of your true eternal nature, you may sometimes grasp at temporary satisfactions and successes to fill your soul's longing. However, deep within your being you hold a sense of the bigger picture of your life – a picture that may need the canvas of your entire lifetime to fill in. And as you say, the only way to get there is from here. But if here is in your heart, then here is a magical place. Here is where you can time travel to heal the past and make quantum leaps and bounds into your future. For here, in heart-presence, is where the eternal meets both yesterday and tomorrow to change everything with love.*

*It is your heart that holds the agenda of your soul. Thus, the more you move through your everyday world heart-first, the more in tandem you will be with your soul-purpose. Be victorious rather than victim. Be not just a survivor of your history, but reborn unto a new life. Say the yes of acceptance to each circumstance that comes your way and receive its gifts – even if you are on your way to creating something entirely different than what is before you at that instant. You will triumph one way or another, sooner or later, in all your endeavors when you triumph in love today.*

*And know this, in kindness and forgiveness for yourself – you may or may not arrive at where you thought you wanted to go, but you will always come to where you need to be. And I, LAUVIAH, and all your Angelic companions, will be right here with you, lighting an unfolding path to the triumph of living life in a way that only you are born to. Amen...*

**4/1** * 6/15 * 8/29 * 11/10 * 1/20

# 12 HAHAIAH

(ha-HA-ee-YAH)

***Refuge, Shelter*** (G)

*'One who is a beacon of shelter within'*

Archangel ~ RAZIEL

Taurus / Mars (5/16-20)

---

## I AM THAT WHICH...

*provides a continual grounding refuge within the soil of your inner life as you are branching out and blossoming into your world. All of life moves in cycles of ebb and flow, sowing and reaping, coming and going, contracting and expanding. You must have roots, or you will be blown about by the seasons of life and the winds of change that always come. Yet we suggest that your deepest roots not be in any person, place, thing or doing, for if these are lost you will be cast adrift. Your perennial roots must be in the depths of your own heart, entwined with the Divine Itself that has planted particular qualities of Its light-beingness within your soul, to be expressed in a way no other can. Your commingled Divine-Human Self is your true refuge, in this and any wonder or way of expression. Return always to this fullness of your true nature, and you will be sheltered by the inner living light that is with you wherever you are, whatever else may come and go.*

*There will be times when you become world-weary and feel the need to retreat in order to recharge and rejuvenate. Give this kindness to yourself. Learn what you need and when you need it, because it takes much energy and courage to brave the seasons of living – in the best of circumstances. Know that ultimately, your surest and safest shelter is not in protecting who you are, but increasing who you are. Learn to say yes to yourself by saying no to the world at times. Learn to choose without guilt, to be yourself without shame and to live without regret or self-recrimination. You will not need to protect your past or your future if you live with integrity and kindness today.*

*I, HAHAIAH, am given to be here within you so that when your light feels dim, you may call on our Angelic hues of unwavering Love to envelope you with our commingled radiance. In this way you will always have enough within and enough to go around. And so come dear one unto this warm cradle of inner light that is always here for you. And be gladdened to share the warmth and comfort of your heart-refuge with those who seek, that they might also remember how to feel and find their own inner hearth-light. Be each other's refuge as we of the angelically Divine are yours. So may it be. Amen...*

**4/2** * 6/16 * 8/30 * 11/11 * 1/21

# 13 YEZALEL

(YAY-za-LEL)

***Fidelity, Loyalty and Allegiance*** (G)

*'One who keeps faith with the inner Divine'*

Archangel ~ RAZIEL

Gemini / Sun (5/21-25)

---

I AM THAT WHICH...

*helps you to be loyal firstly to your soul-self in all things, understanding that the physical expression of your soul is an expression of the Divine on Earth. When you realize that the Divine dwells within you, as you, this puts a whole different light on the concept of 'putting God first,' because God, in this understanding, is not 'out there' somewhere, separate and judging of you. What God actually is and desires for you is so much more personal to you than can be interpreted or understood by any other individual, tradition or dogma wherein you are encouraged to put first what others may 'secondhandedly' re-present God to be.*

*While there is comfort and helpfulness in group perspectives and agreements, no representation or interpretation of the Divine is more personally relevant to you and your purpose as That Which calls from within the altar of your own heart. Consequently, at times, Love and Truth broadcasting from within may call you to a 'road less traveled' that takes you away from the comfort and friendship of the known. And though the way at times may seem to be a wilderness of uncertain, lonely or difficult terrains, know that it is your inherent courage and love of Truth which has called you forth. Keep faith with these treasures of your heart, and you will receive all that you venture to find – even when you don't yet know what that is.*

*I, YEZALEL, say to you: As long as you are loyal to what's on your inside, the way out will be made for you and with you by That Which loves you unconditionally and forever as a precious irreplaceable part of Itself. Understood in this light, you will always be putting the Allness first, and all else shall surely be added unto you. Amen...*

**4/3** * 6/17 * 8/31 * 11/12 * 1/22

# 14 MEBAHEL

(MAY-ba-HEL)

***Truth, Liberty and Justice*** (G)

*'One who is freed by Truth to set Truth itself free'*

Archangel ~ RAZIEL

Gemini / Venus (5/26-31)

---

I AM THAT WHICH...

*helps you to realize the paradoxical nature of 'Truth' as both absolute and relative, universal and personal, One with infinite expressions, a constant that is always changing and expanding. The only absolute, whole or 'true-Truth' is the ever-evolving commingled Love and Truth of the Divine I Am, that is thus not fixed but fluid. This is because the Divine Itself, the author and isness of Truth, is always moving and evolving in response to the movements and evolution of Its creations – so that even Truth itself is continually freed to become a new Truth. Like all relatings between Heaven and Earth, the whole Truth – as opposed to any claims of an 'only truth' – is full of paradoxes that cannot be defined or contained by any one definition or dogma. Truth, because of Love, will meet you wherever and whoever you are, in whatever vocabulary, on whatever path or not, to speak and attend to you in ways that are relevant to both the eternal isness of your soul as well as its expression through your humanity in this particular lifetime.*

*There are layers of meaning to the saying 'the Truth shall set you free.' When you live by the Truth in your heart, the world's ways and relative truths may come and go around you without your being possessed or bound by them. Ultimately, in your willingness to live your personal truth, you set Truth itself free to evolve more and more of its totality through you.*

*I, MEBAHEL, hold light-space within your heart for your personal Truth. As you explore the mysteries of all worlds – inner and outer, seen and unseen – follow what triggers your feelings. Take every piece of new information that comes to you and hold it up to our commingled truth-light in your heart. Give it the intuition and feeling 'sniff-test' to discern its authenticity and relevance to your purpose, what you want and who you are at your deepest levels. The true-truth for you is always the one that sees who you are and, because of love, makes of you even moreso. Ultimately, it is only through the creation energy of love that the whole truth of you, or any, may be revealed and increased. Therefore, dear truth-seeking one, know that if you would truly find truth, then you must love. Amen...*

**4/4** * 6/18 * 9/1 * 11/13 * 1/23

# 15 HARIEL

(HA-ree-EL)

***Purification*** (G)

*'One who uses the light to wash clean'*

Archangel ~ RAZIEL

Gemini / Mercury (6/1-5)

---

I AM THAT WHICH...

*helps you to reestablish communication with your eternal sacred Self in order to purify your thoughts, attitudes, desires, motives and actions so that they may come into greater alignment with your heart-truth and soul-purpose. The purity of your Divine nature is conveyed from Spirit unto your soul and through your heart to radiate throughout your whole being. Although religions and cultures often set standards of purity against concepts of sin and the 'weakness of the flesh,' purity as seen through the Love and Light of the Divine is about acting from a trueness of heart for the highest good. It is expressed through authenticity of feeling, thinking, being and doing without artifice, pretense, hidden agendas or ulterior motives. Purity is evident when the beneficent light within you is shining outward, when there is no conflict between your intent and your actions, between what you mean and what you say, between who you are and what you do. Purity does not imprison, constrain or impose upon you, but frees you into joy and peace and the lightness of being 'all of a piece' – at one with yourself.*

*My light as HARIEL is given to hold a purity-space within you. In those times when you feel contaminated in some way, let the energy of purity that I resonate give you the humility to be recalled unto your inner light and to kneel down in the wonder of communion with your inner Divine at the altar of your heart. Here your thoughts, attitudes, desires, motives and actions may be washed clean so that they come into greater alignment with all that is true in you. Here in your heart of hearts you may be reborn – again and again – from the light within you as a light unto the world. Amen...*

**4/5** * 6/19 * 9/2 * 11/14 * 1/24

# 16 HAKAMIAH

(ha-KA-mee-YAH)

***Loyalty*** (G)

*'One who aligns with the inner Divine'*

Archangel ~ RAZIEL

Gemini / Moon (6/6-10)

---

I AM THAT WHICH...

*helps you to be in mutual loyalty with the Divine that dwells within you and expresses through you and as you, so that you may follow the ways of love and truth as they beckon to you in different times and circumstances. To tell of the Divine's loyalty to you is to say that never in any way will It act to undermine or detract from you. To do so would undermine Itself and the ongoing creation of Itself through you. For you are conceived and born, sustained and ever renewed from the nature and essence of the Divine I AM. As it has been said so simply and truly, 'God is always on your side' – 'your side' meaning the unique choice of experiences that you desire for the expression of your true nature.*

*You and the Divine share the same will and purpose for you – that you may realize the truth of your own 'I Am' as a Divine-Human being, and then through love, evolve and expand that truth of yourself into being and expression. The ways you may do this are your choice, and you do not defy the 'will of God' by choosing one way over another. Choosing is one of the perks of being human! You are expected to choose while you are here – so 'to thine own self be true,' 'do it your way' and 'follow the road less traveled' that only you, in your uniqueness, can take. That is what makes your life interesting – not only for you, but for us and all the cosmos!*

*Thus, to be loyal to the Divine that dwells within you, through you and as you, is to be loyal to your true self and the truth of your own being and purposes. From this high perch within, choose your worldly loyalties. Stand pure in your values and principles – not so that they are unmoving or unforgiving, but with a flexibility that serves caring and compassion rather than fear, exclusivity or judgment.*

*There will be times when you must tear your worldly loyalties away from what would betray that which is true and pure within you. It is then when I, HAKAMIAH, and all the Angelically Divine, may bring light to your difficult hours and remind you that you are still and always all-one here with us, within you. Be sure, despite the seeming at times, that you will not be friendless in your world, for those who are also loyal to their own true withins will recognize you and seek you out as peer and companion. Amen...*

---

Governs on 1/24 simultaneously with 17 LAVIAH

# April 6 – April 13

---

## Angels 17 – 24

---

*Sephira 3*

## BINAH ~ Understanding

*Overlighting Archangel*

**TZAPHKIEL ~ 'Beholder of the Divine'**
Understanding of self and God, contemplation, meditation and compassion

---

**17 LAVIAH**
**18 CALIEL**
**19 LEUVIAH**
**20 PAHALIAH**
**21 NELCHAEL**
**22 YEIAYEL**
**23 MELAHEL**
**24 HAHEUIAH**

**4/6** * 6/20 * 9/3 * 11/15 * 1/24

# 17 LAVIAH

(LAH-vee-YAH)

***Revelation*** (R)

*'One who parts the veil'*

Archangel ~ TZAPHKIEL

Gemini / Uranus (6/11-15)

---

I AM THAT WHICH...

*helps you to recognize the cosmic truths and great mysteries of life through the revelations given to your heart from your soul and its connection to Spirit. Great knowledge and spiritual revelation has always been passed to individuals and the generations of humankind through co-creation and communication among the seen and unseen realms. You have access to our world through your inner hearing, seeing, feeling and sensing. We come to you in many ways – through intuition, the 'small voice' within, visions, the presences of the natural world, coincidental and unusual encounters. You also have access to the eternal realms through the inspired creativities of art, music, writing, speaking and exploratory sciences, as well as the universal languages of symbols, patterns, numbers and colors that represent and transmit light-codes of consciousness.*

*Revelation is thought of as something coming to light which has been hidden, but nothing is really hidden when you truly desire to see. All the mysteries are shining forth their clues in plain sight for those who have a heart-desire to know. What is more often hidden is* ***you*** *– hidden in hurt or regrets about the past or worries and what ifs about the future, which take up so much space within you. However, it is the present, with its portal to the eternal, where* *all is revealed – and the part of you that is most able to come into the present and see and know and feel everything within and beyond is your heart. This is where I, LAVIAH, and all the Angelic Energies of the Divine, wait to share with you whatever you desire to know. So come unto your heart and join us in the circle of our joined light. Let us tell you the story of how you came to be and why you are here and what your Divine-Human life is all about, before and after all. Amen...*

---

Governs on 1/24 simultaneously with 16 HAKAMIAH

**4/7** * 6/21 * 9/4 * 11/16 * 1/25

# 18 CALIEL

(KA-lee-EL)

***Justice*** (S)

*'One who sustains cosmic laws for all'*

Archangel ~ TZAPHKIEL

Gemini / Saturn (6/16-21)

---

I AM THAT WHICH...

*helps to clarify the origin of true justice not as judgment meted out by a separate fearsome God, but rather the dynamics of the universal laws of nature in which all things and beings inherently seek balance within themselves and among each other. What you call the 'Absolute' is not fixed, but kinetic – and not judging, but supportive of exploration and learning. Truth is not immutable, for All That Is is always in movement, always changing in order to move life and creation forward through the cycles of expansion and contraction. As with the ebb and flow of the oceans and the seasons of living in which things and beings come and go throughout the cycles of time, equilibrium must be continually re-established. This is what justice is about – returning the parts to a center of balance so that the whole, even in movement, will always be seeking co-creative harmony.*

*In your world, the birthright of free will coincides with the forgetting of your true spiritual nature. As a result, there is a continual push and pull between extreme polarities and middle ground as you strive to know and fulfill your purposes and potentials. In the dualities of life that propel and compel you in many different outer directions, choices are sometimes made which undermine your own well-being and that of others. Humanity therefore undertakes to police itself with systems of judgment and punishment. However, we of the Angelic realms can see the day when all of humanity has shifted its inner and outer ballast so that all choosings by and among individuals arise from a heart-centered beingness. And then, justice will prevail from within, self-regulating and cooperative, to honor the birthright of a just and fulfilled life for all.*

*I, CALIEL, am the Angelic prompt within you to remind you that you are cosmically justified by your very existence and by your soul as a spark of the Divine Itself living and breathing within you and as you. And because your heart is the broadcaster of your soul to mind and body, being and doing, it is thus the sacred altar of your heart where you may come to know the inner Divine that awaits your recognition within. For truly, it is your heart that knows you are here to manifest the potential of Heaven on Earth through your love, compassion and kindness. It is your heart that knows what is just for yourself and in your interactions with others. And it is your heart, in the service of your soul, that longs to offer your unique gifts and talents unto the world. And so my light as CALIEL is given to shine the way back to your heart through the forest of your worldly concerns. For here in your heart, you may remember your true nature, your precious worth and your rightful and just place and purpose on this privilege of Earth as a Divine-Human being. Amen...*

**4/8** * 6/22 * 9/5 * 11/17 * 1/26

# 19 LEUVIAH

(LOO-vee-YAH)

***Expansive Intelligence & Fruition*** (G)

*'One who uses heart to quicken soul memory and mind'*

Archangel ~ TZAPHKIEL

Cancer / Jupiter (6/22-26)

---

I AM THAT WHICH...

*helps you to draw from soul-memory and the patterns of past events and experiences to inform and quicken the present with greater awareness and the fulfillment of potential. All that happens in your life is a gathering of seasons and cycles unfolding your purpose, including knowledge and experiences that are still seeds in the soil of your being, lying dormant within you until the time of their fruition comes to term.*

*Your heart is the altar and communication 'hub' where the exchange of information and energy occurs between the inner Divine and your humanity. Cosmic memory holds a record of the eternal beingness of your soul and the experiences of all your lifetimes. As your experiences in this lifetime are being 'registered' by your soul and conveyed to the entirety of Spirit and cosmic consciousness, so too may you draw upon cosmic memory and mind to expand your human memory and the range of your intelligence. As you allow this greater intelligence to flow into all your parts, the consciousness of each part is elevated and quickened toward its fruition.*

*As your intelligence aligns more and more with Divine Mind, you understand that you can put a seed in good soil with optimum light and water, but you cannot make it grow faster than it naturally wants to, or it will develop an inherent weakness – like the poorer quality of a food that has been grown in a forced way. It is the same thing with people and ideas when you say that something or someone seems to be 'forced,' which causes a shaky foundation and weakened integrity. All of life is about co-creation, and optimum fruition always involves mutual respect and support for what is needed for the ripening of each and all in their natural time. You see this in how a farmer respects the time needed for each growing cycle from cultivation to harvest, and how ultimately a well-tended farm ripens the wisdom of the farmer.*

*The more your intelligence is imbued with Divine Mind, you come to know that the universe is a great web of co-creation in which all things and beings are interconnected in the manifestation of Divine energies, forms and functions throughout time and eternity. I, LEUVIAH, and all your Angelic cultivators and quickeners, are here to help you know your place and purpose in this great web of life by revealing how the patterns of your life fit together to create the whole that is you, within the whole that is All. Understanding this is one of the greatest foundational functions of your intelligence and is key to furrowing pathways for your fulfillment and fruition. So may it be. Amen...*

**4/9** * 6/23 * 9/6 * 11/18 * 1/27

# 20 PAHALIAH

(pa-HA-lee-AH)

***Redemption*** (G)

*'One who restores the self'*

Archangel ~ TZAPHKIEL

Cancer / Mars (6/27-7/1)

---

I AM THAT WHICH...

*helps you to practice the true and loving principles of redemption by reclaiming yourself from things and actions that are not of your true nature and which disturb the sense of unity that is your soul's reality. As you become more aware of the play of cosmic laws in your human life, you will be able to discern the effects of high and low desires and actions, as well as the power of transformed feelings to change your attitudes, behaviors and life experiences. 'High' desires and actions are those which uplift you and make you feel joyfully alive with a magical feeling that the Universe knows, feels and supports you. Low desires and actions can blind you to the love and light within and around you and others until you feel numb to life, numb to your unique gifts and estranged from the resources of your own heart, where your salvation lies. That said, all experiences on the Earth plane are used by your soul for growth and enlightenment.*

*Cosmic laws are not about rules of behavior, but the interconnected, responsive and co-creative way the universe works – for example, how energetic resonances attract (expand) and repel (contract) each other and how each thing, thought, energy and vibration begets more of itself. These laws are put into play by your thought patterns – but most potently by your emotional being and the feelings that you harbor and emanate. You can choose to think differently, but your feelings must support your thoughts for transformation to occur. Still, start wherever you can. Sometimes, when your heart is hurting you must begin the healing journey by first working with your thoughts and behaviors. It is a way of working from the outside in, until you can reach the inside where true transformation occurs.*

*And so I, PAHALIAH, encourage you with the utmost love – one way or another, come unto your heart where feelings can be healed and changed, for here is where the truth of you is. And here is where we who are of the Divine realms meet you with a Love-Light that is greater than any darkness of hurt, disappointment, shame or guilt you might have ever experienced. Let yourself be reclaimed and restored to an integrity of being and doing by this redemptive Love-Light, which is not something to be earned, but simply received. For this light has never lost sight of your innate goodness and your secret hope that being truly who you are will enable you to give something of value unto the world. Amen...*

**4/10** * 6/24 * 9/7 * 11/19 * 1/28

# 21 NELCHAEL

(NEL-ka-EL)

***Ardent Desire to Learn*** (G)

*'One who inspires delight in learning'*

Archangel ~ TZAPHKIEL

Cancer / Sun (7/2-6)

---

I AM THAT WHICH...

*amplifies in you a natural and passionate desire to acquire knowledge and to explore the mechanics, meanings and origins of things as an exploration of the universe itself. Your enthusiasm for learning is a reflection of the Divine's desire to learn about the further wonders and capacities of Itself through you and your own creations. As you learn, so do we of the unseen realms and all that is Divine. And as artists, students, parents and creators of all kinds particularly know, that which you or others create often becomes your teacher. Is not your knowledge and understanding enhanced by great writings or works of art? Do you not learn more about your own capabilities by the things that challenge you? Do you not learn from the natural curiosity and delight for learning displayed by your children? So it is with the Divine Creator and Its great delight in seeing what more you continue to make of your original making!*

*Learning is often about remembering what you already know at the soul level and bringing it into your conscious awareness, and ultimately manifestation. When you feel a passion for learning certain things, it is often because they are related to your soul purpose. Thus, pay attention to what you are drawn to. Love what you want to learn – even before you know what it is – because that love will give you an all-access pass to its nature and workings. For when you love, you become present, you listen, you respect what is before you and take in its revelations without judgment. The thing itself quickens and expands because your interest and attention draws it out. Even things, because everything is inherently a form of energy, are to some degree sentient and responsive. And thus, no-thing can resist being loved and listened to – even becoming more than it was because of your attention. In so doing, you are co-creating with the thing you want to learn, and soon that which you are learning is teaching you more about yourself as well!*

*Learning gives your life vibrancy – and also makes you interesting to each other – and to us! This is why the energies of the great Tree of Life are a two-way stream of exchange – so that we might bring the infinite 'information resources' of the Heavens to your earthly being and endeavors – and so that all which you are, learn and become here on Earth may also be experienced and 'learned' in the Heavens. Therefore, you are learning not only for yourself, but also for your Angelic allies and all things and beings Divine – as well as for the collective consciousness of all humanity.*

*So I, NELCHAEL, say please do delight in learning – even moreso than any achievement of mastery – so that your life may always have the vibrancy of being receptive to the new or different and the privilege of making the unknown known. And though it may take the world longer to see and commend your achievements, know that in the Angelic worlds you are already and always seen and applauded more for what you are willing to learn than what you already know! Amen...*

**4/11** * 6/25 * 9/8 * 11/20 * 1/29

# 22 YEIAYEL

(YAY-ah-YEL)

***Fame, Renown*** (G)

*'One who seeks knowing of self'*

Archangel ~ TZAPHKIEL

Cancer / Venus (7/7-11)

---

I AM THAT WHICH...

*helps you to realize that the desire to be known by others is often rooted in the desire to know yourself, and more deeply, even subconsciously, to feel known by That Which gave you life. Your human longing to know the who-what-why of the self propels the dynamics of your relationships, creations and purposes from the time you are a small child beginning to explore your world. Deep down, no matter what you discover and create of your world or yourself, or how much you seek and find reflections of yourself in relationships (or not), the feeling persists that there is more to you somehow. And you are right, of course. There is so very much more to you, in fact, than you can experience in this one life. But you can know, and you are here to know, all you need to know about yourself to come into fruition during this life.*

*All of your urges and longings to know yourself and to be known by others are 'echoes' of the first desire of the Divine Oneness to know and see and feel what it was. And it was this great desire that motivated the Oneness to differentiate into the multitude of diverse forms and beings which enabled It to know what it was and be known – and also what more it might become through the life and creativity of Its creations. Thus, as a soul-spark of the Divine within human beingness, you are 'holographically imprinted' with this same urge to seek knowledge of yourself in the other and in your own creations.*

*I, YEIAYEL, am given to help you become known to yourself and the world as a natural result of your true being and doing. And so, be free of concern about yourself in order to get on with joyfully expressing your true passion and purpose in co-creation with your inner Divine. Love what you do more than your need to be recognized for it. And finally, know this – whatever anyone thinks they know about you, or what you may think you know about them – all the renown or fame in the world will not reveal the whole truth of any. Only love can do that. And that is why you will ever be more 'famous' than you already are to the Divine within. Amen...*

**4/12** * 6/26 * 9/9 * 11/21 * 1/30

# 23 MELAHEL

(MAY-la-HEL)

***Healing Capacity*** (G)

*'One who shows where healing is possible'*

Archangel ~ TZAPHKIEL

Cancer / Mercury (7/12-16)

---

I AM THAT WHICH...

*helps you to remember that you were born from wholeness and you may draw from the universal energy of wholeness at any time by attuning your heart, mind and body to the eternal soul within you, which is a spark of the Divine Itself and your lifeline to the Spirit and Origin of your totality. All the physical components of your body are designed to work perfectly in tandem with each other to maintain proper functioning and to 'recalibrate' when needed to sustain harmony. However, your physical being is very reactive to feelings and thoughts. Thus, although you are physically designed to be able to withstand a lot of temporary 'buffeting' about, long-held wounded or disturbed feelings and thoughts can fragment and weaken your physical state and cause impaired functioning and susceptibility to illness and disease.*

*Almost every soul comes into human life to heal the effects of past events, what you call 'karma,' in order to more fully express the 'dharma' of soul purpose and service to others. One of the opportunities of illness is that because it disrupts your present quality of life, it brings you into the present, which is the only time and place healing happens. Thus, illness is essentially a soul-level choice to expand your awareness and to show you where healing is needed at deeper levels. Look to your hurt or illness as a symptom and a sign-pointer, a kind of physical and symbolic 'signature' showing you where imbalance, dis-ease and harbored hurts reside in your thinking and feeling. Look at every happening or condition of your body as an opportunity to receive a gift of awareness, even in the case of 'mechanical' accidents like a broken arm (are you over-reaching or not reaching out enough?), or bumps and bruises from repeatedly running into things (are you distracted or rushed much of the time?), or did you sprain your ankle because you really do need some down time? Or did you or someone you love get a serious illness, perhaps not because of something they were doing or not doing – but something at the soul level that wants to be learned or given. Sometimes even illness is a dharma of service to the self and others.*

*My mission within you is to help accelerate your ability to heal – if it serves your soul-purpose to do so. I, MELAHEL, do this by helping to amplify the exchange of information between your soul, which carries the Divine 'blueprint' for your life potential and purpose, and all the other aspects of your human beingness. Relax your personality identification in time and look inward toward soul-awareness and the memory of wholeness which your heart-wisdom holds. Enter into the light of your totality and look and listen for the gifts of realization. And then be cleansed and restored, in due time, as we in your heart of hearts gladly and tenderly light-assist. Amen...*

**4/13** * 6/27 * 9/10 * 11/22 * 1/31

# 24 HAHEUIAH

(ha-HOO-ee-YAH)

***Protection*** (G)

*'One who is the keeper of true-selfness'*

Archangel ~ TZAPHKIEL

Cancer / Moon (7/17-22)

---

## I AM THAT WHICH...

*helps to strengthen your inner "I Am" that is your built-in protection against inner and outer detractors and transgressions, and which also enables you to value and respect the sovereignty of others. If you are not 'true-self-centric,' you are more likely to be vulnerable to betrayal, disappointment and rejection, the opinions or persuasions of others, and to harbor hidden (or not so hidden) resentment, jealousy, anger or selfishness against others. There is no greater protection against these than being who you truly are, following your own dreams and living your own true life.*

*When you are strong of self, you are more likely to be open, adventurous, welcoming, generous and interested in others. You will not feel the need to contrive boundaries or adopt rituals or tokens of protection. You will have a natural radar for that which is life-and-love affirming, as well as any person or situation that might not have your best interests at heart. It is not that you will be immune to difficulties and challenges, but you will always have the inner ballast of trueness to bring you back to yourself and what matters most. In addition, when you are true to yourself, it is as if you can feel your own 'blip' on the 'cosmic radar' – broadcasting your existence from the place and time where you are so that you might be seen and watched over, known and felt by the universe itself.*

*And so we say, come home to your heart, where I, HAHEUIAH and all your Divine light-relations, remind you not only of who you are – but that you are descended from a Divine lineage so powerful, loving and creative that you have voluntarily chosen to carry a particular part of Its legacy forth from the heavens to Earth in a way that only you can! And because of your willingness and courage to do this, we have come along from within to be your soul-protectors and help you to remember and reclaim your true self and purpose whenever the density, demands, pleasures and pains of Earth life take you too far into forgetting. Thus, above all, trust in the love of the Divine for you, and as you – for love is your true guardian and the guardian of your truth. Amen...*

# April 14 – April 22

---

## Angels 25 – 32

---

*Sephira 4*

**CHESED ~ Love/Mercy**

*Overlighting Archangel*

**TZADKIEL ~ 'Justice of God'**
Mercy and kindness, beneficence,
grace, transmutation

---

**25 NITH-HAIAH**
**26 HAAIAH**
**27 YERATEL**
**28 SEHEIAH**
**29 REIYEL**
**30 OMAEL**
**31 LECABEL**
**32 VASARIAH**

## **4/14** * 6/28 * 9/11 * 11/23 * 2/1

# 25 NITH-HAIAH

(NIT-ha-YAH)

***Spiritual Wisdom and Magic*** (R)

*'One who quickens the abracadabra of life'*

Archangel ~ TZADKIEL

Leo / Uranus (7/23-27)

---

I AM THAT WHICH...

*helps to open your heart to the immense grandeur of Creation and the universal currents and cycles that support life and your own life-affirming soul-song, instilling in you the desire to seek cosmic truths and to cultivate a magical wisdom for living. The natural world is your greatest resource for understanding the ebbs and flows of your own human nature and beingness. Like the abundant seasonal 'magic' of the Divine Energies to seed, germinate, blossom and bear fruit, you too carry this incredible Divine power to enact all the cycles of life within your own unique being and lifetime. The magic of your life is continually perpetuated by the co-creative dynamics of (1) Truth, which is the Divine 'I Am' that is held within your soul, and (2) Love, the creation energy which expands Divine Truth through your personal soul-truth of being and purpose. Thus, these energies of Love and Truth that are within and also around you animate and propel you through the cycles of life in order to help you cultivate your true dreams and purposes, your relatings and relationships, and your Divine-Self awareness that enriches and gives meaning to it all.*

*Life is not an illusion – the only illusion would be in thinking that this life is all there is. Spiritual wisdom brings you the realization that every thing and being matters and has purpose, for life is a time and place venue for exploring and fulfilling potentials that could not be known or happen if all were in a state of physical oneness. Here, in the Divine-Human co-creative magic of physical life, every quality and kind may come into being, fullness and glorious fruition.*

*I, NITH-HAIAH, and all your Angelic lighting assistants, work with great anticipation in the heart-wings of this stage that is your life! What cosmic rabbits will you pull out of your magical-life hat today? What troubles will you disappear into the rarer ethers of love, gratitude and faith? What more of you will magically appear in everything you create? What more will you draw forth of someone else through the heart-magic of love, listening, compassion and kindness? With whom will you populate your personal hall of mirrors to reflect not only who you truly are, but all that you and they might become in friendship and co-creation? Dear one, if you look through our Angel-light you will see that in the spiritual magic of your life, all is so much more than it ever seems, so much more than you may have ever thought possible! Amen...*

**4/15** * 6/29 * 9/12 * 11/24 * 2/2

# 26 HAAIAH

(HA-ee-YAH)

***Political Science and Ambition*** (R)

*'One who inspires cooperative expression'*

Archangel ~ TZADKIEL

Leo / Saturn (7/28-8/1)

---

I AM THAT WHICH...

*helps to bring understanding that on Earth, as it is in the Heavens, the whole is strengthened and expanded by the unique and true contributions of the parts, even as the parts are sustained and replenished by the whole. All of creation enacts and reenacts the patterns and purposes of the cosmos. Ever-repeating cycles of chaos-organization-order are necessary to the expansion and evolution of all life – not only on Earth but in the heavens. The great cosmic order is an arrangement of hierarchies, or 'heavenly collectives,' which recognize and support each according to their attributes, functions and natural aspirations. All of this services the Divine 'ambition' to bring joy and fulfillment to each and all in the ongoing creations of Life, Love and Truth which expand Its own Nature and Presence throughout the universe.*

*You of the Earth compose an important and unique part of the Divine community, for there are cosmic potentials that can only be cultivated and fulfilled on Earth in the dance of individuation and cooperation. There is no greater ambition on Earth or in all the heavens than to fulfill the unique potential of that part of the Divine I AM which you each carry within you. And there is no greater challenge or courage needed to do so than in doing it on Earth. Thus, it is vital for you to have the support of the Divine community in the family you were born into, as well as your communities of extended family and friends, colleagues, neighbors and fellow citizens of your world, that you will continue to build throughout your lifetime.*

*All beings, thoughts, feelings and ideas have an inherent 'ambition' to expand their true nature. Ultimately it will all come down to this: you (as well as your community and greater world) perform most joyfully and successfully when you are doing what you most love – what you are somehow 'built for' or 'born to,' and especially when you are doing that for beneficent purposes with others who share a similar vision. The 'political,' or community, science behind this is in the art of knowing how and where to use your own unique gifts, talents, skills and passions to contribute beneficially in facilitating and collaborating with others toward a stronger whole.*

*You cannot live a full life without including the fullness of your whole self as an inner and outer being. Thus, my role as HAAIAH, and that of all your Angelic attendants, is to help strengthen your inner community of Divine allies so that you may bring yourself in wholeness, rather than only in part, to your earthly communities. From the vibrant interaction of your heart and soul with your Divine community, your truest and highest ambitions may form – those in your heart of hearts, the things that matter to you more than matter itself. Amen...*

**4/16** + **17**am * 6/30 * 9/13 * 11/25 * 2/3

# 27 YERATEL

(YEH-ra-TEL)

***Propagation of the Light*** (S)

*'One who grows the light with love'*

Archangel ~ TZADKIEL

Leo / Jupiter (8/2-6)

---

I AM THAT WHICH...

*plants the light-seeds of higher consciousness in the 'humus' of your humanity so that you might be a light-bearer unto the world, not only shining forth our commingled light from within you, but also disseminating our light in togetherness with others. In the beginning, before the great 'Let there be Light,' there was darkness, or the seeming absence of Light. No-thing was visible because the Light and all things were inside the One and were the One. The energy that engendered Light was Love. For in the Heavens, as it would ultimately be in all of Creation, it is the desire of Love to know the True I AM that a thing or being is made of and to 'bring it to light' through relationship and movement. Light therefore, emerged as the shining child that is born from the commingling of the Love and Truth which is the nature of the Divine Itself. And in the great expanse of emerging Light was illuminated the inherent diversity of the Divine throughout all the cosmos in the hierarchies of the heavens and all of life. Thus are all the hues of the Divine reflected in the diversities of 'hue-manity.'*

*While this is a very simplistic rendering of 'in the beginning,' what we wish you to know is that your soul, as a spark of that Divine Light, is here to further define, magnify and disseminate the legacy of that first Light. And to do that, you must love yourselves and each other and cherish that part of the Truth – the Divine I AM – that you each carry within you and as you. Love and Truth have the highest vibrations. Either of them cause the increase of the other, and their proof of working in tandem is light. Recall how you speak of someone in love as if they are 'lit up' or have a 'glow' about them. Or how luminous you felt or were observed to be when in the presence of love – whether through a person or a passion for something you love to do, create or speak about. Or the stories of beings who have transcended earthly consciousness for a time and report encountering a great light from which emanated the presence of a boundless unconditional love that knew them truly and completely? These are glimpses of your Love and Truth light-nature and origin.*

*There are as many ways to love as hearts willing to do so, and as many ways to compound love as those joining their hearts with others through listening, caring, compassion and acts of kindness and concern. No matter what 'bushel' it may seem is over your head or around your heart at any moment in time, your light is always within you, awaiting your own willingness to shine forth the love and truth of yourself. Know know that this is true for others as well – and so when you shine your light upon them, you help to quicken their own.*

*So I, YERATEL, say go forth in love and truth to propagate our joined light among you. Know that my Angelic light within the well of your heart is evidence of the great Love that the Divine truly has for you, and from which you may endlessly draw forth for yourself and others without the supply ever being diminished. For Love and Truth compose the light-stuff of the Divine Heart which increases with every partaking and every giving, on Earth as it is in the Heavens. Amen...*

**4/17**pm + **18** * 7/1 * 9/14 * 11/26 * 2/4

# 28 SEHEIAH

(say-HAY-ee-YAH)

***Longevity*** (G)

*'One who extends life with creation energy'*

Archangel ~ TZADKIEL

Leo / Mars (8/7-12)

---

I AM THAT WHICH...

*represents the 'Great Healer of the Zodiac,' helping you to align with the cosmic template of wholeness and continually siphon the creation energies of the Divine for the renewal of your being. Your soul, as a unique spark of the Divine, is eternal. Paradoxically your sometimes wish to 'live forever' has already been granted with your cosmic birth, for indeed, the soul-light within you is living forever! However, in the context of time, your soul voluntarily submits its eternal reality to the physical paradigms of a human life-span in order to explore and experience Divine-Human co-creation in ways that only life on Earth provides.*

*In physical life, all aspects of your being must be well-fed: your body needs nourishing food; your heart needs love and a sense of personal truth; your mind needs consciousness, 'food for thought' and productivity; and for 'soul-food' you need both communion with the Divine and the manifestation of earthly meaning and purpose. All these 'foods' which nourish your Divine-Human beingness help to feed the fires of creation energy and the new inner and outer constellations of you which they forge. In every moment of your life you are being energized, enlivened and created anew through the replenishment of cells in your physical body and the spark of new mental and emotional stimuli that give you opportunities for greater awareness and the cultivation of heart-wisdom. And all of it is propelled by the spiritual energies that are continually funneled from Spirit into your soul and from there to your heart and the whole of your being.*

*It is natural for all the parts of you to work in tandem with these creation energies to accomplish your continual renewal. I, SEHEIAH, am here to support you in doing so – by shining a light upon all that is life-affirming within and around you, and helping you to course-correct and heal when you make choices that can diminish or impede your life-force. As your Angelic inner ally, I invite you to identify especially with your soul-reality when your physical reality becomes challenging or difficult – because your soul reality holds the memory and template of your wholeness. Your soul helps you to remember, humbly, that you choose difficult circumstances at times so that you might accelerate your learning. However, with self-love and compassion, learn to measure everything and everyone that comes your way against the soul-light of your own intuition and heart-wisdom, and choose what you will. For that is your birthright. Amen...*

## **4/19** * 7/2 * 9/15 * 11/27 * 2/5

# 29 REIYEL

(RAY-ee-YEL)

***Liberation*** (G)

*'One who liberates the love and truth of you'*

Archangel ~ TZADKIEL

Leo / Sun (8/13-17)

---

I AM THAT WHICH...

*helps to liberate your soul into tangible expression in time and place for the birthright of your fulfillment and that of the Divine that dwells within you – and at times to free your soul-consciousness from its physical confinement so that you may be inspired to new heights. Here is the paradox of your Divine-Human life: an all-knowing soul which lives in the forgetting of the flesh, sojourning voluntarily on Earth as an 'angel without wings' who still yearns for the heavens. You know that being human is a privilege because there are potentials of Love and Truth that can only be manifested in life; yet the fulfillment of these require both a forgetting and a remembering of your eternal soul nature. The forgetting stimulates the creativity of your human self, but inspiration brings back the remembering of your soul self and its limitless ability to create. Thus, you need the freedom and inspiration of both the forgetting and the remembering, without being bound by either.*

*I, REIYEL, am here to free you to walk between the worlds of forgetting and remembering. By helping you to cultivate a sense of emotional non-attachment to the tides of daily happenings, you can be free to partake of the spiritual energies and opportunities that underlie and propel them. And so come with me today to step away from your world of time and place to visit the eternal and utterly free 'off-world' that is your energetic Source. Here you can soothe the thirst that is often unquenched in your world. Here in this eternal realm is the Love and Truth of who you are in your greater reality, without the yoke, and yes, opportunity, of seeming lack or need – only ever-expanding possibility. Be here for a little while of timelessness and be filled. Breathe in the boundless light-elixirs and be lightened. And when you are ready, return to the world of time to free yet more of that greater light into this life and what it yearns to become through you, for you and as you. Amen...*

**4/20** * 7/3 * 9/16 * 11/28 * 2/6

# 30 OMAEL

(O-ma-EL)

***Fertility, Multiplicity*** (G)

*'One who loves life into being'*

Archangel ~ TZADKIEL

Leo / Venus (8/18-22)

---

I AM THAT WHICH...

*helps you to tap the infinitely fertile and creative nature of the Universe that is inherent in you and all your desires, ideas and imaginings, conceptions and inceptions, life energies and creations. Creativity is a natural attribute of every living being because inherent in all beings is the creative light-stuff of the Divine Itself which desires to increase and multiply. As the Divine brought you forth from the inherent diversity of its own Oneness into the uniqueness that you are, you carry the 'image and likeness' of the Divine nature within your own soul-spark. Through you and your own creations, the Divine comes to know what more it might become. Likewise, as you convey your own beingness unto that which you create, you come to know what you are made of and what more you might become. And so the generations of creation throughout time convey and express the expanding Oneness through Divine-Human co-creation and the multiplicities of infinite becoming.*

*The fertility to bring forth life from within you, in one form or another, is always present. There may be times when you feel physically, emotionally, mentally or spiritually barren or dry – without ideas, thoughts or optimum conditions to bring forth creations. However, it is not that you are not fertile, but that perhaps on a soul level your fertility wants to take a different form than the one you have envisioned or are trying to 'force.' Or, you may be full of fears, worries or doubts that are blocking the flow of creation through you. Or you may be in a context, atmosphere or collaboration that has a diminishing effect on your creativity.*

*True creation energy does not deplete, divide or take away from you. For in the giving of yourself to bring forth life, your own essence is multiplied, amplified and increased. You become more than you were and a part of you lives in the new birthing. This is true whether you create a child, a poem, a picture or a beautiful environment. In the act of creation, it is love which calls essence into form. To draw on the creative omnipotence of the Creator Itself, you must create what you love and love what you create – even when you do not yet know what or where it is or how it may be brought forth. For when you beckon something into being for love's sake, the love you birth it with shall be reflected and multiplied in the thing born to show you more of who you are and what more you are capable of. This is exactly what you do for the Divine Itself within you and in the greater reality of Oneness that is your cosmic womb.*

*And so I, OMAEL, and all in the Angelic realms, bring the light of the Creator to all your creations so that you may become a unique co-creator within the All, contributing to the beautiful diversity of Oneness by the life you have loved into being. Celebrate this fertile creative glory within and of yourself as we and all the cosmos experience the expansion of the Divine through the wonders of your own glorious creations. Amen...*

**4/21** * 7/4 + 5am * 9/17 * 11/29 * 2/7

# 31 LECABEL

(LAY-ka-BEL)

***Intellectual Talent*** (G)

*'One who puts all the pieces together'*

Archangel ~ TZADKIEL

Virgo / Mercury (8/23-28)

---

I AM THAT WHICH...

*translates the vast nature of the Divine into your human faculties so that you may understand the inherent interrelatedness of diverse beings, things and systems and how to tap the vitality of talent and co-creativity among them. Whether a thing is a piston, a plant or a person, no one part within any of these functions alone. Like your saying, 'it takes a village,' every thing or person performing at its optimum does so with the vitality of collaboration among its inner and outer parts and associations with others. As you access the blueprint of Divine Mind imprinted within your own human mind, you will understand that the Universe does not work through finite events of random chaos. Your greatest intellects are visionaries, with the ability to see the patterns of interconnectedness that dance in the co-creativity between the inner and the outer, essence and form, the unseen and the seen – and how two seemingly different kinds of things or beings can be complementary and completing rather than opposing.*

*The key to grasping all of this is in the wisdom of your heart, which knows that you cannot comprehend the whole if you isolate one part to the exclusion of the others. It is your heart that brings art and soul to your intellect, giving meaning to what your intellect wants to make sense of. Take, for example, your arts and sciences.*

*At the heart of scientific and mathematical formulas is the beautiful art of evolving patterns with numerical and conceptual components that affect and effect each other. Without art and meaning, science would be an intellectual exercise that would always just miss its greater potential to reveal the nature of the universe. Likewise, without artistic tools fashioned by science and your technologies, certain art forms would not have the means to convey their wondrous inspirations. Without heart, the head would suffer a relentless ache of thoughts, figures and facts without feeling, meaning or purpose. Without mind, heart would be without focus and form to give meaning time and place. Without feet, heart and mind would have no ground to stand on from which to launch dreams up and over the gravities of fear and logic.*

*And I, LECABEL, can assure you that without the ever-evolving potential of you, we of the angelically Divine realms would not be able to experience the wonder of what more is possible in the universe because of your heart's longing for a life that matters, the talent of your mind working with all your parts and the contributions of all, seen and unseen, to help you bring it about! Amen...*

**4/22** * 7/5pm + 6 * 9/18 * 11/30 * 2/8

# 32 VASARIAH

(va-SAH-ree-YAH)

***Clemency and Equilibrium*** (G)

*'One who balances judgment with mercy'*

Archangel ~ TZADKIEL

Virgo / Moon (8/29-9/2)

---

I AM THAT WHICH...

*brings the mercy that tempers judgment and restores balance, without which true justice and a return to harmony would not be possible. The universe is naturally just – but it is not fixed. Thus, in the universal tides of ebb and flow, contraction and expansion, justness is achieved by the renewal of balance – and so, it is the nature of every thing and being in Creation to seek balance. Since life is always in motion and 'for every action there is a reaction,' balance is something that must be continually restored during movement. Without mercy, judgment can degrade into vengeance and chaos. Without judgment, mercy can degrade into immorality and mayhem. Working together, mercy and judgment create justness and justice, which always seek to return an extreme situation or behavior to harmony and equilibrium.*

*You experience this need for tempering and balance in many life scenarios – such as disciplining your children in ways that teach rather than hurt them, giving someone more time or favorable conditions to pay a debt, weighing an appropriate sentence against someone who has committed a crime while taking into consideration the possibility for rehabilitation, or giving loved ones leeway for their hurtful actions by recognizing that they themselves are hurting. Compassion and righteousness work together to create healing, growth and a return to balance, so that something new and productive can be born from past acts. This is a reflection of how Love and Truth are forever balancing the universe itself. Each not only tempers the other, but inspires new contexts and 'constellations' of co-creativity that enable each to become even more of itself by the presence, contribution and cause of the other.*

*I, VASARIAH, tell you that the best of your relatings and relationships have at their heart this mystery of equilibrium through co-creativity! You are here together to both temper and inspire each other and to thus increase your individuation so that you might ennoble and expand the whole. In this way, may you do unto yourselves and each other what is done for and with you by the Divine Itself, again and again, for the ever-evolving love and truth of you. Amen...*

# April 23 – April 30

---

## Angels 33 – 40

---

*Sephira 5*

## GEBURAH ~ Strength & Judgment

*Overlighting Archangel*

**CHAMAEL ~ 'Severity of God'**
(Also CHAMUEL or KAMAEL)
Change, purification and clearing of karma
for stronger loving and nurturing relationships

---

**33 YEHUIAH**
**34 LEHAHIAH**
**35 CHAVAKIAH**
**36 MENADEL**
**37 ANIEL**
**38 HAAMIAH**
**39 REHAEL**
**40 YEIAZEL**

## 4/23 * 7/7 * 9/19 * 12/1 * 2/9

# 33 YEHUIAH

(vay-HOO-ee-YAH)

***Subordination to Higher Order*** (R)

*'One who calls you to higher ground'*

Archangel ~ CHAMAEL

Virgo / Uranus (9/3-7)

---

I AM THAT WHICH...

*quickens the 'Christ consciousness' held within your soul self so that you might come into a right and true hierarchy of relationship with Divine Love, self-love and love of others. If you would 'love thy neighbor as thyself,' you must first love yourself rightly in order to love your neighbor rightly. Often the understanding of altruism in human life values the idea of being 'selfless' and thinking of the other person first, while denigrating the thinking of yourself first as a display of selfishness. Both can miss the mark. If you are really selfless you would be giving nothing away if you don't have a self to give. Being selfish is when someone is 'like a self, but not quite' (as in one you may call childish who is not a child but acting like one), and it results from the need to protect what little of a self one seems or feels to have. We would rather see you be 'full of yourself' – in a state of full and loving SELFNESS – and give that, because that will be a gift that keeps on giving!*

*To be full of selfness is to be full of all the parts that make up a self – the Divine and the Human – and as such to live with the awareness that it is the Divine within you and you within it which has loved you into life and continues to sustain you. If this is your high constant, then whatever you give to others will proceed from that higher love and true caring of the other as the Divine Itself cares for you – and for them through you. You will not need to worry for your own lack or well-being as you give of yourself, because the Divine within you is continually replenishing you with discernment about how, when and what you need to receive. For true 'selflessness' is not giving in absence of the self, but without fear or concern for yourself because you know you are always being loved, watched over and given what you need.*

*In all your strivings, look to the journey rather than the destination, for the awakened soul knows that 'getting there' happens by fully being wherever you are in each moment. Do what you love and you will have soul-success in your every moment, even if worldly success does not come in your time. For in the higher order of life and beingness according to the natural laws of love and truth, 'the first shall be last, and the last shall be first...the meek shall inherit the Earth...the servant shall be the master...and the riches of the heart are greater than those of the pocket. All beings and things in the universe are propelled by love, all natural laws are fulfilled by love – and without love there is only tyranny.*

*And so I, YEHUHIAH, am here within you to illuminate your path to the Divine Love within that you may receive and be embraced by this great Love and know and feel that you are loved utterly. For then what you give to others may be from the treasure of this, your own inner Divine coffers of love, caring and compassion from which you may truly 'love thy neighbor as thyself.' So be it, and truly so. Amen...*

**4/24** * 7/8 * 9/20 + 21am * 12/2 * 2/10

# 34 LEHAHIAH

(lay-HA-hee-YAH)

***Obedience*** (R)

*'One who amplifies inner authority'*

Archangel ~ CHAMAEL

Virgo / Saturn (9/8-12)

---

I AM THAT WHICH...

*helps you to cultivate obedience to the inner authority of your own true will, which is the will of the Divine for you to express the Love-and-Truth of Itself through the love-propelled expression of who you truly are in your own soul purposes and relatings of all kinds. There are many opinions and dogmas formed by humankind about the nature of God and all things Divine. In order to have right understanding of obedience in your relationship with the Divine, yourself and others, there must be healing of any notion that you are at the mercy of the whim and will of a separate, distant, fearsome or even disinterested God. There is no 'higher power' outside of you that is not also within you and you within It.*

*You are composed of a unique constellation of qualities derived from Divine Essence and earthly matter, Holy Breath and human flesh. To be obedient to the Divine is not to obey a separate, above or 'somewhere out there' god that others define – but the God that expresses both the universality and particularity of Itself within you, through you and as you. To obey the God within is to be willing to be who you truly are, not only to fulfill the magnificent potential of your humanity in Earth-life, but also to fulfill the desire of the Divine to experience life in the ways only you can as a Divine-Human being. And thus, as you consent to walk this path of obedience to your inner Divine Nature, you will be more able to truly and rightly choose your worldly path.*

*Above all, I, LEHAHIAH, say to you dear one: keep returning to your heart – for your heart is the broadcaster of your soul, where your inner Divine dwells and wherefrom It calls you. Obedience born of the heart is a discipline of love and purpose rather than guilt or shame, an offering of loving commitment rather than a task of coercion. Such obedience shall not become a rigid dogma imposed upon yourself or others; rather, it shall be a loyalty that is compassionate and malleable to fluctuating needs and circumstances, an allegiance born and sustained through love, and a fidelity to an ever-evolving truth of the Divine I AM that you are an expression of. Amen...*

**4/25** * 7/9 * 9/21pm + 22 * 12/3 * 2/11

# 35 CHAVAKIAH

(cha-VA-kee-YAH)

***Reconciliation*** (R)

*'One who resolves paradox'*

Archangel ~ CHAMAEL

Virgo / Jupiter (9/13-17)

---

I AM THAT WHICH...

*helps to broaden your understanding of seeming opposites in the dualities of earth-life, and to reconcile your own dual inner and outer natures which compose the Divine and Human aspects of your being. Everything in your world operates through relationships between like and complementary things which often manifest as polarities. The dynamics of contrast between dualities such as day and night, black and white, right and wrong, yes and no, what you have as opposed to what you want, and so on, are the paradoxical means which, from the beginning of Creation, have propelled the ongoingness of life that is continually moving itself and you forward. You can see these movements in the ebb and flow of the tides, the birthing-dying-rebirthing seasons of the natural world and in the life cycles of all living beings.*

*The contraction or waning of any one thing enables the emergence and expansion of another. Thus, together, each facilitates, propels and helps to define the other and does its part to contribute to the whole – the way day and night together create the entirety of a 24-hour day, or how the absence/contraction of light (black) is a display field for the presence of light (white). This is how the dualities, or polarities in nature are inherently reconciled to each other: each thing provides a momentum and complementary context for the other – and for everything taken away, something new is given.*

*Likewise, your inner and outer natures of essence and form, meaning and matter, heart-mind-soul and body together compose the full functioning and fulfillment of your Divine-Human being on Earth. No, you are not 'only human!' I, CHAVAKIAH, assure you that your well-being and ultimate fruition depends on your willingness to reconcile – as in acknowledge and live with – this awareness. Your soul, as a spark of the Divine, is like your pre-installed life-long battery. It powers everything in your inner and outer life. If the contact points are not aligned, you will be running on only a 'partial charge,' and thus your power will be weakened.*

*Your heart is the hub that connects your soul with the rest of you, so the quickest way to understand what your soul needs is to consult your heart and its soul-indicators – your feelings, intuitions, personal truths and wisdoms. Allow your heart to weigh in with how you live your life and move through your world, and you will have your best shot at a fulfilled and joyful life. Not that you won't have challenges, but you will have all your inner resources on tap to deal with them – including us, your inner Angelic light-mates who are the amplifiers of your own soul-light into your heart and all the other parts of your being.*

*Dear one, embrace the wondrous totality of yourself, knowing that although you may have been told that you long ago left the 'Garden,' the Garden is still within you – and it wants to grow. Amen...*

**4/26** * 7/10 * 9/23 * 12/4 * 2/12

# 36 MENADEL

(MEH-na-DEL)

***Inner/Outer Work*** (S)

*'One who dances two worlds into one'*

Archangel ~ CHAMAEL

Virgo / Mars (9/18-23)

---

I AM THAT WHICH...

*helps your heart to choreograph the dance of your life as a grand 'pas de deux' between your inner and outer aspects as the two great realms of your beingness on Earth that compose your Divine-Human nature. Your entire being is animated by a unique spark of the Divine that is your soul and which carries a 'hologram' of the Divine Nature and its urge for manifestation and fulfillment of potential in, through and as you. This can only happen in the dance between essence and form, soul and body – and the heart that brings them together. Thus, you might say that your soul has two lifelines that meet at your heart – one connecting you to Spirit, and the other to your humanity. When the ends that meet in your heart are joined together by love and wisdom, your progression through life is like a circle dance from the inner to the outer to the inner, and so on. As your human 'ego' identifies more and more with your inner Divine I AM, your consciousness spirals higher and higher and your doings on Earth manifest ever more meaning and purpose.*

*Your heart holds the agenda for your soul on Earth. Thus your heart is the hub where the Divine meets and commingles with your humanity in particular ways according to your soul purposes and human needs. Your outer being is composed of all aspects of your physicality, your personality expressions, actions and the details of your worldly moving about. In order for you to live a true, loving and fulfilled life, the inner and outer aspects of your being must be working together in a continual two-way exchange of energy, information and awareness. Yes, we know how compelling the outer world is and how much you are naturally influenced and affected by its delights and demands and the commonly held beliefs about what constitutes a 'normal' and successful life. However, when you interface with the world in a conforming stance much of the time, you can forget the treasures hidden within your inner being that contain your true soul-self and your most unique and valuable offerings for the world.*

*Thus, I, MENADEL, and we light beings all, are your Angelic dance partners, here in the ballroom of your precious heart where your inner and outer meet, poised to teach the Divine and Human parts of you how to dance together in the most exquisite, loving and dynamic pas de deux in the universe! They are playing our light-song, dear one – shall we give it a whirl? Amen...*

**4/27** * 7/11 * 9/24 * 12/5 * 2/13

# 37 ANIEL

(AH-nee-EL)

***Breaking the Circle*** (G)

*'One who lifts you out of the circle into the light'*

Archangel ~ CHAMAEL

Libra / Sun (9/24-28)

---

I AM THAT WHICH...

*helps you to harness the transformational cycles of the natural world in order to stimulate healing and rebirth, as in nature's capacity for regeneration after a prolonged period of infertility, deluge or aridity. The circle of life progresses through seasons and cycles of birth, growth, harvest, dormancy, death, fertilization, gestation and rebirth. In the human life span these cycles happen on physical, emotional, mental and spiritual levels. For a new cycle to successfully begin, the current cycle must either be broken open or made whole so that it will release you.*

*As humans, you need beginnings and endings to feel that you are making upward progress along a circle of life that moves like an ascending spiral – rather than the kind of circle that seems to keep taking you back to where you started. You must know, however, that the seeming repetition of scenarios and 'circling back' is usually not a 'backsliding.' Even if it does sometimes seem that you are returning to the same place, what is always different and greater is you – now ready to address something which has come to the surface that was not ready to emerge before. It is much like the way all healing happens: that which is most apparent is dealt with first, which opens the way for the underlying things to come to the surface. And they will, for everything that is out of balance or hurting wants to be healed.*

*Some learning and healing happens instantly, and some happens slowly – according to what best serves the totality of you. Know that despite the desires and impatience of your personality-self, your soul-self truly has your best interests at heart! Every time you are frustrated or disappointed by how long something seems to be taking, consider what additional gifts are still in front of you that are asking to be received.*

*All that said, there is another way to break out of the circle – a kind of quantum leap to another level. And that is through self-love, forgiveness and compassion. Any of these three graces, which originate in your heart, will trigger the other two. No thoughts, dogmas, rules or rituals, pushing or pulling can accomplish this miracle. It is about coming to the innermost altar of your heart, where you are met by the Divine Energies in a deeply personal way that attends to your particular pain and longing, your beautiful and unique potential and your inherent purity as a child of the Divine. Therefore, come within, unto us, for I, ANIEL, and we Angels all, have been given to meet you in this healing moment and help lift you out of the circle of time's limitations into the light of your greater beingness and ever-emerging potential. Amen...*

## **4/28** * 7/12 * 9/25 * 12/6 * 2/14

# 38 HAAMIAH

(ha-AH-mee-YAH)

***Ritual and Ceremony*** (G)

*'One who enlivens the path with love'*

Archangel ~ CHAMAEL

Libra / Venus (9/29-10/3)

---

I AM THAT WHICH...

*helps you to enliven rituals and rites in order to germinate the light-seeds of the Divine within your human beingness so that what is 'Above' (inner) may be manifested 'Below' (outer). The 'above' on Earth resides in your inner essence and consciousness, and the 'below' is expressed through your physical form and your outer being and doing on Earth. This inner-outer dance between the Divine and the Human is the exquisite choreography that moves your life forward into meaning and fulfillment. Rituals are meant to get you onto the 'dance floor' – not to leaden your feet or deaden your heart to the music of life and its mysteries. As long as rituals, rites and ceremonies propel feeling and meaning, they can trigger the bursting forth of the light within you.*

*When dogma, mindless repetition and over-familiarity cause ritual to lose its potency and cease to enliven and revitalize you, we urge you to reinvigorate your practice or cultivate a new one. Come back to your heart – to the feeling and even the longing that the true use of ritual intends to fulfill. Let your heart be receptive and malleable to the light seeking rootedness within you, and become utterly present so that you may feel the inner Presence desiring communion and expression of Itself through you.*

*As you invite the inner Divine to inhabit the outer movements of lips and limbs that compose your ritual, feel the breath of God breathing you in and out and out and in with the words spoken or the song sung. Feel how your beingness is authored by the Divine Itself and carried out through your willingness for a Divinely-inspired and fully-lived life. Feel the love that engendered you and continues to watch over you from within and all around. Let this love be magnified to fill the sounds and scents and scenarios of your ritual, remembering that truly, there is nothing that is not of God. Even the glory of the rising sun and ribboned dawn is a daily cosmic ritual – and it is all for you! So bring me, HAAMIAH, from your light-endowed heart into your own personal devotional, so that love may be brought to life through you, for you and as you upon your daily paths of words, wisdoms and ways. Amen...*

**4/29** * 7/13 * 9/26 * 12/7 * 2/15

# 39 REHAEL

(RAY-ha-EL)

***Filial Submission*** (G)

*'One who honors what was while inspiring what will be'*

Archangel ~ CHAMAEL

Libra / Mercury (10/4-8)

---

## I AM THAT WHICH...

*helps to carry forth and reflect the energetic hierarchies of the heavens through the succession of generations in Earth-life. Coming into this life, you are as a new blossom on the Divine-Human Tree of Life, carrying forth both the 'spiritual DNA,' or essence, of your Divine origin, as well as a unique version of the physiological makeup of your human ancestry. In both essence and form, you are an offspring of all that came before you – even as you have been endowed with new variations that hold the potential of what more you can make not only of yourself, but of the Divine and earthly parents who engendered you.*

*'Filial submission' benefits both what came before and what will be. It is not for you to bend or mold yourself to prior authority, but to acknowledge and draw upon that authority's experiences and strengths and fold them into your new formations. Without you the Divine cannot experience Earth-life or what more can be made of It by your unique configurations and variations – and you cannot reach your full human potential without drawing upon the presence and power of your inner Divine. In the case of your human parenting, your life makes something more of theirs as you carry forth that which can be expanded upon and leave behind what is no longer needed.*

*As for us, your faithful light-relations, we love to experience through you what more can be made of all that the Divine has endowed you with of Itself! Through you we can touch and feel, see and smell, taste and savor, hear and speak the next newness of life! How you delight and enliven our realm with your being and doing! How you transport and magnify us when you tap our energies within you to allow us to co-create with you! And likewise your earthly parents and ancestors, in their true heart of hearts, delight in what more you make of yourself as you draw upon what they too have given you. Bow down to these gifts, and then stand up with the strength of them to reach for the sky of your own new dreams and doings. And know that I, REHAEL, and all your light-companions, await here within you with a shimmering of love to give your heart loft and lightness so that you might fly your being, and ours, into bold and beautiful new becomings! Amen...*

**4/30** * 7/14 * 9/27 * 12/8 * 2/16

# 40 YEIAZEL

(YAY-ah-ZEL)

***Divine Consolation and Comfort*** (G)

*'One who is a soft landing for your heart'*

Archangel ~ CHAMAEL

Libra / Moon (10/9-13)

---

I AM THAT WHICH...

*helps you to enter the comfort of the Divine that is within you, within others, and between and among you, and especially to feel welcomed and consoled when the world seems for a moment to be disappointing or to cast you out or leave you behind. From afar we can truly only imagine and observe how hard it must be to be human – to have your great power and knowing continually muffled, veiled and confined to physical form and time-memory! To be shuttled between life's ebbs and flows and pulled into the whirlpools and undertows of emotions that are both a blessing and a challenge to your humanity! Though these things are natural and sometimes necessary to the progression of your soul-growth in Earth-life, we know that they are often difficult and painful. But from within you, we can feel what you feel, and because of your willingness and courage to be on Earth, the compassion that is our nature overflows.*

*So, I, YEIAZEL, am here to offer you an Angel-shoulder for leaning, a wisp of feathery lightness to dry your tears, a sky-full of Divine heart to cradle your disappointments, and winged Love to fly you away to the sweetest reveries and new imaginings. Always, always you may come within and be received and restored to help you 'go back out there' when you are ready. And may you also do for each other what is done for you herein. Be each other's soft landings of presence, comfort and listening, and feel when an embrace is kinder than a word or more loving than a solution, and when to just be is the sweetest rest from the perennial becoming that the outer world both offers and demands. Let the world wait sometimes – for it will always be there. But you will only have this moment to be here. So let time give way to foreverness and let us hold you in the presence of this eternal moment and breathe the breath of light for you this little while, in the way you breathe life into those you love by your listening and holding them within the cradle of your heart. Amen...*

# May 1 – May 8

---

## Angels 41 – 48

---

*Sephira 6*

## TIPHARETH ~ Beauty, Harmony

*Overlighting Archangel*

**MIKHAEL ~ 'Who is as God'**
(Governs with RAPHAEL*) Power and will; ignites strength, courage and protection for spiritual seeking and healing

---

**41 HAHAHEL**
**42 MIKAEL**
**43 VEULIAH**
**44 YELAHIAH**
**45 SEALIAH**
**46 ARIEL**
**47 ASALIAH**
**48 MIHAEL**

* Note that the Archangel correspondences in Sephirot 6 and 8 have been interchanged throughout the centuries by different Kabbalists and schools of thought. After additional research which shows the ways in which both Archangels are active in both Sephirot, the primary Archangel correspondences presented in the original *Birth Angels* book are reversed here, but each are included as co-governing.

**5/1** * 7/15 * 9/28 * 12/9 * 2/17

# 41 HAHAHEL

(HAH-hah-HEL)

***Mission*** (R)

*'One who brings Heaven to Earth'*

Archangel ~ MIKHAEL (with RAPHAEL)

Libra / Uranus (10/14-18)

---

I AM THAT WHICH...

*helps you to cultivate and express the true Christic spirit of universal love, compassion and forgiveness for self and all so that you might advance unencumbered toward your full purpose for being. Christic principles are not origined in or exclusive to Christianity, but precede all religions as the nature and expression of Divine Love for all of creation from the beginning of time. Your histories are peppered by transcendent souls who have incarnated at crucial times to embody and remind humankind, each in their way, of this Great Love. For it is this Love that brings meaning to all you are and all you create, without which would render you and all of life as empty husks and pantomimes of possibility.*

*Every person on Earth has the same 'bigger picture' mission and reason for being, each with your unique means of expression: to cultivate the heart of the Divine in your own so that Love may take root on Earth within and among you. Thus may you flower and come to fruition in all your unique potentials and purposes as an expression of the Divine I AM within your human form. And as the fruits of your love-labors release their light-seeds to the Earth-winds of time and change, they will have the strength and the power to seed ever more expressions of love – compassion, kindness, forgiveness, generosity, gratitude – and the willingness to allow others to be as they are, without judgment, knowing that Love comes to each and all in the way, time and place most true and beneficial.*

*For Love is not hard or fixed, but soft and malleable. Love obeys no laws and yet fulfills them all. Love gives all that it is, and in the end has more that it started with. Love is boundless and infinite, yet takes the shape of whoever receives it. Love knows not only what a being is, but who it longs to be. Love knows that everything and everyone is nothing without it, and so gives itself unto every no-thingness so that it may become all.*

*I, HAHAHEL, and all that is Divine, are here within your innermost altar – your heart of hearts, where we are always sounding the steady rhythm of Love that continues to bring you and the truth and ways of your purposes into greater and greater beingness. Let your mission be to use Love, receive and give Love until it has soaked you through and you become Love! Amen...*

**5/2** * 7/16 * 9/29 * 12/10 * 2/18

# 42 MIKAEL

(MIH-kah-EL)

***Political Authority and Order*** (R)

*'One who helps you find your guiding light'*

Archangel ~ MIKHAEL (with RAPHAEL)

Libra / Saturn (10/19-23)

---

I AM THAT WHICH...

*helps to illuminate the laws of Heaven (above) in play upon the Earth (below) and within the inner and outer priorities and hierarchies of your humanity so that you might align with your own inner 'guiding light.' Cosmic laws are energies proceeding from the natural order of the Divine Itself disseminated throughout the cosmos, which are also expressed through the soul (eternal) and body (temporal) natures of your Divine-Human beingness. As humans, you often suffer for things that 'happen' to you – but every happening is related to a cause that has to do with the ways in which energies relate to each other. There is no authority in the Divine realms that desires to punish you for anything. All exists to bring you more and more into awareness and co-creation with your inner Divine so that you might become whole and fulfilled within yourself and contribute to the wholeness of all.*

*Cosmic laws are not static, but always advancing the purposes of Divine Love and Truth according to the diverse expressions of the Divine Nature within humanity. Just as there is a primordial, or originating, energy that guides the universal order of things, so must there be some guiding principle, or context, at the helm of your own human beingness. For example, the context that literally gives your soul a 'leg to stand on' is your physicality. Without physicality, your soul purposes cannot be fully viable or applicable on the Earth plane. In terms of what you do with your life here, you must make certain choices in their order of importance to guide your decision-making. For example, is it most important that you have a job making a certain amount of money, or is it most important that you have a job you like, even love? Is it more important to be married because it will enhance your economic or professional stability and bring community acceptance – or is it more important to find someone you truly love? These sorts of things are not oppositional or mutually exclusive, and you could have them all – but there is a hierarchy of priorities as to how and why your choices are exercised in what order, and this order affects the overall quality of your life.*

*Do you have a guiding principle or personal navigation system with a 'home' button that returns you to what matters most when the road of your life sometimes takes you far afield? We don't mean a static, unmoving rule or dogma that you obey no matter what – but a fluid constant that can bend to the winds of change, ride the tides of ebb and flow – and still be there as your inner barometer and ballast when circumstances and people in your life change and come and go, or you are faced with difficult choices.*

*Only you can determine your higher authorities, but we suggest in terms of finding or creating those to consult, of course, your heart, where what matters most to you is rooted in feeling, personal truth and the search for a meaningful life. Here in your heart is where I, MIKAEL, and all our Angelic relations, 'hang' with you, so if you would like our help in this, dear one, here is where you will find us. Amen...*

***

While many of the Angels' messages refer to cosmic laws in different ways, I thought it might be helpful to have a brief summary of those that are most noticeably at work and play in our human energies and life events. And as you'll see, they all involve interactions within the paradigms of duality and relationship.

**The Law of Correspondence**: As it is above, so it is below; the Heavens are a template for Earth and Earth is a reflection of the Heavens – just as each part of our inner and outer Divine-Human nature mirrors the other.

**The Law of Resonance (or Vibration)**: Everything is in movement and vibration because everything is composed of energy; like vibrations attract each other – just as we naturally attract what our core beliefs, desires and attitudes are resonating. (This is also called the Law of Attraction.)

**The Law of Polarity**: Everything has a seeming opposite in order to create contrast so that the universe may continue to expand; however, polarities are simply two complementary manifestations that together facilitate and compose one thing – like two sides of a coin, the light and dark that comprise a full day, or masculine (assertive) and feminine (receptive) energy.

**The Law of Cycles**: Everything flows in and out through cycles of contraction and expansion, which are the movements that brought forth creation and continue to do so – like the ebb and flow of the tides, the seasons of nature and the cycles of birth, death and rebirth.

**The Law of Cause and Effect**: In the planes of manifestation, duality prevails, thus: for every action there is a reaction; every cause has an effect and from every effect is born a new cause. This underlies consequence and the importance of doing toward another what we would have them do toward us because we 'reap what we sow,' even generations later.

**The Law of Balance (or Karma)**: Because like attracts like and we reap what we sow, disruptions and distortions seek a contrasting movement in order to return to equilibrium. Thus any previous actions which caused imbalance or harm return to us in order to experience the effects of the actions we committed and also to be able to heal the effects of those actions. Thereby we are able to restore balance and harmony to the present by "cleaning up" the past.

## **5/3** * 7/17 * 9/30 * 12/11 * 2/19

# 43 VEULIAH

(vay-OO-lee-AH)

***Prosperity*** (R)

*'One who shines the light of possibility'*

Archangel ~ MIKHAEL (with RAPHAEL)

Scorpio / Jupiter (10/24-28)

---

I AM THAT WHICH...

*helps you to enter into the flow of universal abundance which is unlimited and always welcoming and available to you as you are willing and able to receive. In the universal realms abundance flows as a river of endless resources for any to partake of. However, this constant flow is so light that you may not always feel its ever-present fluidity in the density of the Earth-plane; thus, that same river of plenty on your side of the 'veil' can sometimes seem to be more like a gossamer filament in the wind, or a swamp full of geysers and sinkholes!*

*There is much over-identification on Earth with the 'haves' and 'have-nots' – and the idea that abundance is a 'luck of the draw,' 'here one day, gone the next' or that there's 'not enough to go around.' It may seem that prosperity, of any kind, is withheld from you at times, or all the time, causing you to identify with a sense of lack or feel that the universe is fickle and unaware of your needs and desires or that you are undeserving in some way. None of that is true.*

*Abundance is not a matter of deserving, but desiring – and answering your desire for abundance is one of the ways life moves itself forward and continues to expand through you. However, if your deepest belief about yourself is that you cannot have prosperity, even though you may sincerely desire it, your negative belief will either keep prosperity from reaching you or cause you to squander your resources on ignoble purposes. Even so, the solution is not to fight against seeming scarcity, but rather to create an inner atmosphere of prosperity to which riches of one form or another will be drawn – unless you have chosen the context of scarcity in some part or time of your life, for some particular soul-growth.*

*True prosperity is about receptive thought, feeling and being – and it shows up in your perspectives, your attitudes, behaviors and circumstances. Money is only one form of prosperity – but it happens to be the one your world is most consumed with. It is a common thought among you that heaps of money and possessions are necessary to have a good life. But this is based on a mistaken notion that the more you acquire, the happier you will be. The only way that concept can be true is if you are in the heart-and-soul business of acquiring joy, friendship, love, meaning, purpose and all such things that cannot be measured, bought or bartered. All these things are free, and you can have as much as you want!!! The secret to getting these treasures? Giving. You may not get back what you've given from exactly where you gave I, but because of the law of resonance, whatever you give outwardly will be returned to you multiplied from somewhere or someone. In addition, as you extend love, friendship, meaning and purpose, these things reshape your inner being on their way out to the world.*

*In the meantime, I, VEULIAH, say – if you want love, be love. If you want friendship, be a friend. If you want joy, be joyful. If you want meaning and purpose, let your heart be the guiding presence in your life. For here the voice of your soul waits to be heard at any moment you are ready to listen. Here, 'where your heart is, there shall your treasure be.' Amen...*

## 5/4 * 7/18 * 10/1 * 12/12 * 2/20

# 44 YELAHIAH

(yay-LA-hee-YAH)

***Karmic Warrior*** (R)

*'One who heals the past by loving it.'*

Archangel ~ MIKHAEL (with RAPHAEL)

Scorpio / Mars (10/29-11/2)

---

I AM THAT WHICH...

*helps you to understand that true victory over the karma of unhealed issues belongs to those who win the battle that cannot be fought, for karma is not a thing to vanquish, conquer or be punished or defeated by. It is rather an opportunity for healing the past by loving and accepting it – thereby changing its effect on the present and enabling the parts of you held hostage by the past to come into the present and start anew. The paradoxical mystery about the present is that it can bring you into the presence of the eternal, and the presents/gifts the eternal offers to your human life in time. These eternal gifts will show you the totality of your true nature and enable you to feel how much you are loved, and that indeed love has never left you because you are made of love. And by this love you will see that all which has occurred in the history of your soul within human form and context has been a gift to bring you to the higher ground of unconditional love and compassion for yourself, and ultimately others – even as you are so loved by the Divine and all the Angelic beings who continually attend your soul upon its every sojourn into life.*

*Thus say I, YELAHIAH, to you: Accept your past, knowing that 'that was then, and this is now' – and the gift in now is healing. Allow yourself to love again. And to be loved. For it is love that heals the past and love that gives your present the future that belongs to you. And dear one, allow us to help you endure the challenges of your healing journey with courage and integrity. And especially, may we help you to open your heart in willingness, which conjures within and around you the Angelic energies of love and lightness of being that inspire quantum leaps in the graces of healing and at-onement. Amen...*

## **5/5** * 7/19 * 10/2 * 12/13 * 2/21

# 45 SEALIAH

(say-A-Lee-YAH)

***Motivation and Willfulness*** (S)

*'One who fires your heart-motor'*

Archangel ~ MIKHAEL (with RAPHAEL)

Scorpio / Sun (11/3-7)

---

I AM THAT WHICH...

*helps to fire-up the motor of your heart with a passion for life, love and co-creative living that is fed by the Divine fires of inspiration and the flow of Divine Love as a vital life fluid through all your parts. You can do anything you want on the Earth-plane – but that is often just the quandary – what do you want? And why? What is your motivation? Your will and motivation must be supporting each other in order to yield something that has true value for you and others. But first, we wish you to understand this: your own true will is an extension of – not different or separate from – the Divine Will that you carry out your soul purposes toward the fulfillment of your unique human potential. Period. You are not here to give over your soul-will to some distant or hearsay god, nor to your neighbor, your lover, your friends, family or colleagues.*

*It is the nature, opportunity and responsibility of your soul, as a spark of the Divine, to fulfill its Divine potential within your human beingness. And only with this understanding will your motivation be aligned aright for manifestation that is true to and for you, as well as beneficial to others. Right motivation does not involve taking things from others in order to satisfy only oneself – but rather inspiring and co-creating with the wills and ways of others so that the potentials of each and all might be compounded and magnified.*

*So here's a clue for right motivation: what you truly want is connected to what you love – for in your heart of hearts, having to do or be anything else will always be a pale imitation of the 'real thing.' Remember what you love, what you were naturally drawn to as a child or developing adult before the world or who-you-thought-you-should-be prescribed something else for you. Remember what you love, and let it inform and enliven or even change the work you do into a purpose to be fulfilled. And then watch how that which you love calls forth the totality of yourself from all your life experiences and heart's desires, including little quirks and hidden talents. Even forgotten pieces of you will return that were once left behind somewhere because they were too painful to keep carrying without giving them time and place in your life choices.*

*I, SEALIAH, say to you dear soul-manifestor: Remember what you love and let love re-member you and all your parts. Remember your true self – which your soul, and all that is Divine, has never lost sight of. We are here, in your heart of hearts, to help bring you all the way into the world. Too late, you think? Hear our resounding Angelic 'no!' In love's eternal world of now, it is never too late – and if not now, when? Amen...*

## **5/6** * 7/20 * 10/3 * 12/14 * 2/22

# 46 ARIEL

(AH-ree-EL)

***Perceiver and Revealer*** (G)

*'One who demystifies the mysteries'*

Archangel ~ MIKHAEL (with RAPHAEL)

Scorpio / Venus (11/8-12)

---

I AM THAT WHICH...

*helps you to discern and illuminate for others the mysteries of Divine Thought and Being hidden in human consciousness and the patterns and paradigms of earthly life. Clues to the secrets of life are as close as you are to yourself. It is common for your awareness of the Divine within your nature to become dimmed in the dense vibrations of Earth life. Therefore, it is my light-task to help you see how the longings in your humanity and the details of daily life are both reflections and clues of cosmic patterns and universal truths at play within you and your place and purpose in the bigger picture of your life. Through understanding these things, you can begin to solve the greatest mystery of life – the paradox of your Divine-Human nature and why your inner is always vying for expression in your outer life – not only for your own sake, but for those in your world and in the cosmos.*

*How to begin to approach these mysteries is the obvious question, to which the answer is always: begin with your heart, and take it with you wherever you go – in fact, to borrow from human cleverness, 'don't leave home without it!' The Divine Nature is composed of the commingling of Love and Truth, and it this that is carried within your soul and imprinted in your heart of hearts as feelings, intuitions and personal truths. Feel what there is to feel, without prescribing what you 'should' feel, and let your feelings lead you into revelation, meaning, motivation and a sense of purpose propelled by love.*

*Thus, you may unlock the keys to the ever-evolving mysteries through your heart and its remarkable powers and capacities for love, compassion and the discernment of truth in everything and everyone you encounter. And as for the transmitting and sharing of what you discover, I, ARIEL, and all your Angelic allies, suggest doing that from your heart too. You may be a 'Lion of God' and want to roar your truth-findings out into the world, but then be lion-hearted! For a great loving heart makes every truth you offer go down so much easier – like the sweet cherry in cough syrup! For any truth is only a half-truth without the greater knowingness of Love. Would you want love to tell your story, or truth? Either of them without the other would only tell part of anyone's story. For together, they tell not only who you are, but who you long to become.*

*And so finally, we wish for you to realize that the only One Truth on Earth is that it would take the totality of humanity and all the beings in all the universes to reveal and realize the Whole Truth that is composed of the many within the Oneness. So please do relax the limitations of exclusive thinking, dogmas and belief systems, and enjoy the unfolding of life and the gifts of revelation that come to open hearts and minds. Let there be light and joy within you – and the wisdom of understanding that each mystery revealed is yet another glorious glimpse and clue to All That Is within you, and you within All! Amen...*

**5/7** * 7/21 * 10/4 * 12/15 * 2/23

# 47 ASALIAH

(ah-SA-lee-YAH)

***Contemplation*** (G)

*'One who sees the patterns and purposes'*

Archangel ~ MIKHAEL (with RAPHAEL)

Scorpio / Mercury (11/13-17)

---

I AM THAT WHICH...

*helps to draw you into your depths and heights so that you might see and feel the 'cosmic template' which inhabits and propels all the inner and outer parts and purposes of your own and all beings – as well as the seasons, cycles and consciousness of the Earth itself. Contemplation is about 'bringing Heaven to Earth' by offering yourself in receptivity to the Divine which is manifesting aspects of Itself through your humanity. Since receptivity is key, you can be drawn into contemplation during the stillness of meditation, prayer, writing and creative work, reading or listening to music, sitting or walking in nature, and so on. As your time and frequency of contemplation increase, you will more and more resonate with the patterns of Divine Presence that configure all aspects of life.*

*The more you feel and experience the mysteries of your inner Divinity, the more you will understand who and why you are. In the totality of your Divine-Human beingness, you are here to co-create and focalize particular aspects of the cosmic template according to your unique nature within the 'greater scheme' of all life. Though you may have epiphanies of sudden insight or awareness during contemplation, it is the practice of contemplation over time that gently and surely raises your energetic vibrations and your awareness, so that in a kind of 'slow-*

*cooker' way you are more and more able to be that which contemplation allows you to see, know and feel.*

*Ultimately you may approach all your life doings from that contemplative space within you, which will allow you to perform your purposes and tasks with more awareness, mindfulness and a sense of interconnectedness with all beings, things and circumstances – and also especially with the beautiful Earth that sustains you. I, ASALIAH, am honored to be your Angelic guide to illuminate these paths of exchange between your inner Divinity and your outer humanity so that your totality may become one grand field of play for the great 'game' of Heaven on Earth! Amen...*

**5/8** * 7/22 * 10/5 * 12/16 * 2/24

# 48 MIHAEL

(MIH-a-EL)

***Fertility and Fruitfulness*** (G)

*'One who taps the light-elixirs of life'*

Archangel ~ MIKHAEL (with RAPHAEL)

Scorpio / Moon (11/18-22)

---

I AM THAT WHICH...

*helps to bring forth abundant life through creativity and creation in all life forms on all levels of being and doing. Creation by its very nature is infinitely fertile, bringing forth the fruits of that which has been seeded in due time if inner and outer conditions have supported growth and blossoming. Just as the life force of a single daisy can draw it up through a crack in stone, anything or anyone with a compelling desire for life will find a way to live – in one form, way, time or another. In human life, optimum conditions for growth might be a nutrient-rich atmosphere full of love and kindness, encouragement, education and opportunities. Even in the seeming absence of these, however, fields of flowering success may blossom if desires and endeavors are fed by the stream of a clear and fertile mind and the well of a willing and determined heart. No matter what your outer circumstances, when you draw from your inner 'taproot' into the eternal, you gain access to the resources of love, inspiration and light-support that empower you to create a different outer reality.*

*Creation energy, which is sourced from the Divine Itself and Its own first act of Self-Expression, is programmed into all of life and is self-generating. Thus there is no such thing as 'not being creative.' Creativity yields many forms and has many purposes –*

*all of which serve the expansion, expression and regeneration of life. Therefore, being creative is about aligning with the creation energy already within you in a way that is natural to your nature and your desires. In any creative process where there is an atmosphere of awareness and full aliveness,* ***attention*** *to an idea, desire or inspiration becomes focused into* ***intention and the will to act****. For desire is the primordial 'motor' of the universe that drives materialization, as works are the spiritual and material 'children' of desire.*

*The wonderful thing to realize about creativity of any kind is that the thing you are creating wants to be created and will help you to bring itself into being when you attune with it. Ultimately, of course, what attunement means in the language of the heart is loving – and creation is essentially about 'loving a thing into being' – for it is love that brings forth life and expands the truth of its 'isness.' Love is receptive, awakening imagination and intuition and the inspiriting of ideas and greater knowings. Love makes you present and draws presence. Love enables you to listen and draws the telling. And as you listen and feel, that which wants to be created will draw on your skills, talents and experiences for its formation.*

*It is the purpose of my energy as MIHAEL to quicken the creation pulse within you and to help irrigate the seeds of your ideas and imaginings with the light-elixirs of Love and Truth in the flow of warmth, wonder and understanding. And be assured that all your Angelic muses gather round to contribute when any creating is going on – because we so joyfully love to lend our love-light to co-creation! Amen...*

# May 9 – May 16

---

## Angels 49 – 56

---

*Sephira 7*

**NETZACH ~ Victory**

*Overlighting Archangel*

**HANIEL ~ 'Grace of God'**
Joy, light, insight and true unselfish love
through relationship with the Divine

---

**49 VEHUEL**
**50 DANIEL**
**51 HAHASIAH**
**52 IMAMIAH**
**53 NANAEL**
**54 NITHAEL**
**55 MEBAHIAH**
**56 POYEL**

**5/9** * 7/23 * 10/6 * 12/17 * 2/25

# 49 VEHUEL

(VAY-hoo-EL)

***Elevation, Grandeur*** (R)

*'One who in-spirits the magnificence of the higher'*

Archangel ~ HANIEL

Sagittarius / Uranus (11/23-27)

---

I AM THAT WHICH...

*helps to elevate your experience of life by amplifying your awareness that the 'higher' is within you as your own soul-spark of the Divine. To realize your greatest potential as a human being is to understand and embrace the realization that you are not only human, but a Divine-Human being. God, by any name, is not a separate, impersonal energy that is 'higher' or beyond you – but rather the pervasive and animating essence and energy that dwells within every sentient cell and molecule of your being.*

*When you speak of higher consciousness, you are essentially referring to 'ascension energy,' which, during life, is not about leaving your body but transforming your body and being at all levels with light into a lighter vibration. This is done by drawing forth the energies of your soul, which carry your meaning and purpose in both the cosmic and earthly realms into your* ***heart****, which, in receiving communications from your soul generates love, compassion, intuition, wisdom and personal truth. By tapping these, your body and mind are suffused with greater awareness, and your total being is elevated energetically. Heart and soul qualities vibrate faster because they contain the light that is born of Love and Truth – the essential compositional stuff of the Divine. Body and mind qualities contain more earthy and dense vibrations,* *which are heightened when permeated with light from the awakened interaction of heart and soul.*

*When you create from this higher vibrational energy, you are co-creating with the creation energies of Divine Love, which are limitless. You become able to in-spirit knowing beyond thought, and expand the capacity of your mind to form and communicate what you inwardly receive. With its newly endowed powers and capacities, your mind becomes an enhanced partner with your heart and soul. Drawing from the eternal creation energies, your physicality may even take on a visible glow as your physical vibrations are sped up. Engaging often at this ascended level of being by working at what you love can actually 'youthify' you if you are also giving your body the nutrition, rest and exercise support it needs to withstand and sustain a higher vibratory environment.*

*The 'perk' of all this is that working with the higher creation energies gives both timelessness, universality and presence to your purposes and creations. While there are multitudes of differences in thought, form and expression, there is a sameness of heart and soul across the whole spectrum of humankind in the desire for love, truth, meaning and purpose. Thus, there are few hearts that will not quicken to the higher energies which are captured in great tangible works – especially in poetry, art or music.*

*Therefore, dear inwardly and outwardly aspiring one, I offer you my VEHUEL light with which to paint your lofty inner and outer vistas, to climb higher mountains and fly into dreamed-of horizons that await you. And in the meantime, with every next step feel the lighterness of being that comes when you step a little more enthusiastically, a little more lovingly, a little more truly, higher and braver! Amen...*

**5/10** * 7/24 * 10/7 * 12/18 * 2/26

# 50 DANIEL

(DAH-nee-EL)

***Eloquence*** (R)

*'One who uses words to bring forth life'*

Archangel ~ HANIEL

Sagittarius / Saturn (11/28-12/2)

---

I AM THAT WHICH...

*helps you to tap the spiritual beauty and power of language to inspire and bring forth new life by opening heart and mind, quickening soul-presence and transmitting the enlivening energies of love and truth. The deepest mysteries of sound and word were born with the first utterances of the Divine that brought forth from Itself the Light of Love and Truth that is Its nature into the diverse manifestations of Life. Likewise, words among humans have tremendous power to not only communicate and inform – but also to inspire, heal, catalyze transformation and create bridges of friendship, hope, understanding and cooperation among individuals, families, colleagues and nations.*

*True eloquence is not just a presentation of cleverness or 'a way with words,' but a manifestation of integrity that means what is said and says what is meant. At times, however, no matter how well-intended or committed the sayer, like action does not follow. There can be many reasons for this, but often at the root is your simple saying, 'easier said than done.' In the dense vibrations of Earth-life, it is so much harder to do things than to talk about doing them. That doesn't necessarily make the speaker, or conveyor, any less sincere or what is said any less important.*

*Words of the life-affirming kind are light-seeds. What is spoken of or written in one human generation may not reap fruit until the next or for many more to come. But the words hold energetic space in the collective soul of humanity for your highest ideals, and ultimately they can inspire people to move mountains, even for millennia. So what is the fuel that propels a thought or word to take the whole journey into action and beingness? Again, as with so many questions, the answer is Love – love of life, love for a greater truth, love for the ever-present possibility to bring betterment to all.*

*I, DANIEL, and all the Angelic light energies of the Divine, are within and around you to remind you when you have so understandably forgotten: Let the words pass through your heart before they leave your lips, so that they might take the love within you into the outer world. And thus the words will be known for the energies of love which they release, the seeds they will plant in hearts and minds, and the new growth that will rise up, sooner or later, to inspire a more loving and meaningful life for any 'who have the heart to hear.' So be it. Amen...*

**5/11** * 7/25 + 26am * 10/8 * 12/19 * 2/27

# 51 HAHASIAH

(ha-HAH-see-YAH)

***Universal Medicine*** (R)

*'One who draws from the Oneness to heal'*

Archangel ~ HANIEL

Sagittarius / Jupiter (12/3-7)

---

I AM THAT WHICH...

*represents the cosmic light-states of wholeness, harmony and balance that are held within your soul and which are ever more accessible as you allow the higher vibrations of your soul-essence to flow into your physical being. In the Divine Angelic realms, where essence is not dimmed or diminished by the density of matter, unity and wholeness prevail. In Earth-life, where beings are composed of both form and essence, seeming duality prevails. The spiritual-physical duality of your nature is sometimes debated as oppositional, but in truth duality itself has a sacred dual and complementary purpose: to give space, contrast and movement for individuation in human life, while giving Spirit a vehicle for palpable experience and ongoing creation. Thus, the paradox of duality is that both aspects of your nature work together to expand the totality of you and the Universe itself.*

*In the meantime, while the dualities of human life provide much opportunity for growth and expression, sometimes it can seem as if you have 'fallen between the cracks,' or gotten stuck 'between a rock and a hard place,' as you put it. Trying to push through the density of physicality and seemingly oppositional things and dynamics can be confusing and frustrating and cause fear, doubt, worry and other clenching reactions which disturb or impede the natural flow. When these effects are prolonged, they can result in stagnation, imbalance and mal-being. But of course there is a cure! All you need is something that unblocks the blocks so that your body and being can do what it does naturally – which is to heal and make you whole.*

*The universal medicine for this paradoxical predicament between your human-encased soul and your soul-animated humanity is the fluidity of Love. For this golden light-elixir is a pervasive 'water of Life' that can run like a stream through every part of every thing and being, all the inners and outers, all essence and form, all thought and beingness, connecting all because it IS All and all is born of it. Love is your original Divine 'stem cell,' and there is nothing it can't transform, cure or make whole.*

*So, I, HAHASIAH, invite you to come within unto the well of your heart and the wonders of your soul and drink your Love medicine – or to borrow another of your sayings – have a little of 'the hair of the dog' (go ahead, spell dog backwards) that birthed you! Amen...*

**5/12** * 7/26pm + 27 * 10/9 * 12/20 * 2/28 + 29

# 52 IMAMIAH

(ee-MAH-mee-YAH)

***Expiation of Errors*** (R)

*'One who makes whole'*

Archangel ~ HANIEL

Sagittarius / Mars (12/8-12)

---

I AM THAT WHICH...

*helps you to correct seeming errors, mistakes, distorted motives and hurtful actions by healing the separation between your inner and outer – your soul-self and your personality-self. All the hurt caused and suffered in Earth-life has at its root the forgetting of who you truly are and being torn and fragmented by opposing desires and continual shame, self-judgment and unforgiveness. Your soul is your connection to Spirit – the Divine, the All, God, Source, Heaven – however you may understand or name your cosmic origin and home. The things of your world are wonderful, pleasurable, seductive, challenging, difficult and more – and when your attention is continually captured by them without having a way or practice to return to your inner and a remembrance of what truly matters to you, you can become imbalanced and lost to yourself for a time. Expiation, or atonement, is simply coming back into balance and at-onement with your own soul-self and the Spirit that is a lifeline for your entire being.*

*My mission here at the 'confessional' of your heart is to receive you and show you how to receive yourself in Love, the cure and correction for all things. Here you may forgive yourself and remember how to forgive others. Here you can reinvigorate your outer life and world of personality and action with the meaning and purpose of your inner life and being. Here in your heart waits the truth of you and the power to heal and transform whatever you bring to it. This is something we do together, you and I who am IMAMIAH, and all that is Divine. Bring us your hurting pieces and parts and we will put you back together again! Amen...*

## **5/13** * 7/28 * 10/10 * 12/21 * 3/1

# 53 NANAEL

(NA-na-EL)

***Spiritual Communication*** (R)

*'One who sends and receives from within'*

Archangel ~ HANIEL

Sagittarius / Sun (12/13-16)

---

I AM THAT WHICH...

*helps you to nurture a meditative disposition and allow times of solitude, rest and inspiration for opening your heart, communing with the inner Divine and drawing on the eternal energies and all-knowingness that increase when you are utterly present with Presence. Spiritual communication is a two-way exchange happening continually, whether you are aware of it or not. We always hear and feel you – but you often think we aren't listening, or you may not consciously hear or feel us because there is so much static on your side of the 'veil' from all in Earth-life that continually demands your attention.*

*We are not within and around you to interfere with your will, but we do have our ways of capturing your attention! Our messages to you are often in the startling encounters and coincidences between yourself and others, and in timely events, 'luck,' conversations, gifts, surprises or help from friends and strangers. We also attend you in illness or difficulty, when you are the most likely to ask for and be willing to receive help.*

*Your soul is 'hard-wired' by its nature to the world of Spirit. Thus, at the very least you are always in communication with us in the background of your daily life – analogous perhaps to an 'automatic back-up' of your feelings, thoughts and activities to a cosmic 'cloud drive.' However, the more fruitful scenario would be to bring our communications more into your conscious awareness for both sending and receiving. As you purposefully communicate with us and invite us to communicate with you, the richer the co-creation between the inner and outer aspects of your being for a life full of love, meaning and purpose.*

*I, NANAEL, want you to know that we receive the most potent communication from you through your feelings. Because of the higher vibrations of feelings and emotions, if you are thinking or saying one thing and feeling another, what we hear are your feelings. This is how human beings often confuse each other – when you pick up on feelings and intent, despite the words or actions. So for the sake of true and clear communication between yourselves and us, we invite you to speak from your heart, so that you will be truly heard – on both sides of the veil! Amen...*

**5/14** * 7/29 * 10/11 * 12/22 * 3/2

# 54 NITHAEL

(NIT-ha-EL)

***Rejuvenation and Eternal Youth*** (S)

*'One who grows the rose of foreverness within'*

Archangel ~ HANIEL

Sagittarius / Venus (12/17-21)

---

## I AM THAT WHICH...

*helps you to draw on the energetic 'hologram' of eternal life and love as the creation energy carried within your soul in order to continually refresh the vitality of your entire being. Humankind's age-old preoccupation with youth and fantasies of immortality are rooted in the fact that a part of you is indeed already immortal. There is a fountain of youth – but it is within you, in the wellspring of your heart which holds your soul-light and from which you may drink the life-giving elixirs of your ever-present inner Divine. Energy and essence are eternal. Within the clay vessel that contains it, the soul which animates your body is the energy of Love fired in the kiln of the Divine Heart, and thus it lives on. Just as your body needs nourishing food, drink, light and warmth to be healthy, what your soul needs is the food of Love, the elixir of Light-consciousness and the heart-fire for a meaningful life.*

*Through the passion and enthusiasm of your heart, you tap creation energy, which rejuvenates all the parts of you – body, mind, heart and soul. When you engage something or someone with the desire to bring forth the love and truth of it, him or her, you are in effect siphoning a drought of the Divine's own birthing elixir which brought forth all of Creation. In the two-way Divine-Human dynamics of creation energy, by your heart-involved engagement with all of life you enliven the Divine within you, and thus you are inwardly and outwardly enlivened, rejuvenated and capable of seeding and blossoming more and more of life.*

*I, NITHAEL, and all your Angelic lights, are the Divine within you from which you may continually recreate yourself with the eternal elixirs of Love and Truth. Eat and drink of us and be filled and fulfilled. Share and shine our bounty with others so that they too might be moved to a draught and taste of the eternal that is within them. And cease any longing for immortality, for you already have it where it really counts! Amen...*

**5/15** * 7/30 * 10/12 * 12/23 * 3/3

# 55 MEBAHIAH

(may-BA-hee-YAH)

***Intellectual Lucidity*** (G)

*'One who feeds clarity from inner and outer streams'*

Archangel ~ HANIEL

Capricorn / Mercury (12/22-26)

---

## I AM THAT WHICH...

*helps to imbue the workings of your intelligence with Divine Thought in order to heighten your awareness, clarify your purposes and magnify your inner and outer qualities to support them. When your soul does not have a body, receiving and comprehending Divine Thought goes much more 'as the crow flies,' because it is simply a transmission of light. However, when your soul is enveloped by human substance, desires, thoughts and emotions of all kinds, as well as a bombardment of outer stimuli, more variables must be listened to and considered. Thus, despite the cacophony of influences and 'noise,' for clear thinking you must weigh information and input from all available resources from the inner and outer streams that are feeding your intellect at all times.*

*The inner stream begins with Spirit, which transmits continual Divine support and guidance to your soul (this is where your Angelic allies come in!). Your soul communicates this spiritual information to your heart, which registers as feelings, intuitions, inspirations and personal truths. At the same time, your own mind is both sending to and receiving from your heart, which serves up a 'chicken-or-egg soup of feelings and thoughts that are constantly stimulating each other. Add to all that the enormous amount of stimuli from your outer world of daily and moment-to-moment relatings and experiences that are affecting all parts of you at once – and you can imagine how much compassion and admiration we of the Angelic realms have for your courage to be human!*

*For your entire life you are drawing consciously and unconsciously from all of these streams and their tributaries. In terms of the outer stream, it can be quite a challenge to discern clearly what to take in and what to disregard or move on from – especially in a world where parents, friends, colleagues, business and commerce may strive to define or influence what should be interesting to you. Of course, from an Angelic point of view, everything in your world is interesting! However, your opportunity and soul mission as a human being is to narrow your field of focus so that you can fulfill your particular agenda of potentials and purposes for this lifetime. You came to Earth to be someone no one else can be: yourself. And as tempting as it may be sometimes to model yourself on other people's expectations or ways of being, there is no skin your soul is going to be more at home in during this lifetime than the one you chose to be here in.*

*And so how do you narrow your focus and achieve clarity? We say to measure all outer information by the discernment that is given through the insights and intuitions that come from your combined inner streams of heart, soul, mind and body working and communicating together. If you are feeling foggy about some decision or course of action, chances are you have forgotten or are disregarding some part of you – which means you don't have all the information you need to make a clear decision. Ultimately, clarity comes from knowing – and owning – what matters most to you, and lining up everything else behind that.*

*And that's why I, MEBAHIAH, am here to help illuminate and guide the meanderings of cosmic and earthly streams to meet up in the ocean of your heart, where what matters most to you resides. If you are still uncertain, we say follow your feelings! And by feelings, we mean the ones that are born from the soul of you that are voiced within your heart, the ones that show you who you truly are and that love and accept you just as you are while you are on your way to becoming yourself even moreso. All the rest of it can be worked out from the clear-seeing of that. So please do use me as your personal Angelic light-spectacles so that you can see yourself as I do, and so that we can both see your unique dreams and purposes set sail with the heart-winds of Love and Truth at your back! Amen...*

## **5/16** * 7/31 * 10/13 * 12/24 * 3/4

# 56 POYEL

(poi-EL)

***Fortune and Support*** (G)

*'One who taps plenitude with feeling'*

Archangel ~ HANIEL

Capricorn / Moon (12/27-31)

---

I AM THAT WHICH...

*helps you to open the well of your heart to awareness of the infinite inner flow of Divine abundance and support that meets all your needs and desires, in one way and time or another, according to your soul purposes. For your whole life, your inner being is trying to get your attention so that you may become aware of and come to rely on the foundational support you inherently possess for your life on Earth. As alone as you ever may feel at any moment of your life – and however persuasive and real that feeling may be – it is not fact. By virtue of your soul, which is a spark of the Divine Itself within you, there is always 'someone at home within.' This does not mean that you don't or won't have times of trial and travail – because these are your own soul choices. The world is compelling, always drawing you outward toward manifestation and experience. And that is good. However, with extended outer focus you forget your soul choices, you even forget your soul – and thus, you forget the power and purpose that lie within you.*

*Your creations and life experiences can become hollow if you lose touch with inner meaning and purpose. And so, as it often goes in life, it is only when the world seems to shut you out or down or away, that you remember to re-turn inward and be in the presence of what gives support and true mattering to your life and to the matter you are so compelled by.*

*Your soul knows that you will have only a partial and unfulfilled human experience if you try to 'go it alone,' without your innermost resources of heart and soul through which all that is Divine supports you. Thus, your soul may choose times of adversity and lack to help you turn inward so that your greater awareness will be awakened and enable your inner Divine to 'populate' your human aspects and adversities. And even when your soul chooses to use a seeming limitation of resources as a context for growth, when you have learned what you desire to learn through lack, you will see that at the horizon of your awareness awaits all you need.*

*With greater awareness, you come to understand that lack is also a phase in the natural cycles of contraction and expansion that propel life and all things and beings forward. When the flowers disappear in the fall, do you hang back to mourn them or move on to enjoy the fruits and harvests that follow? And when those wane, do you not revel in the brilliant colors of fall leaves and invigorating crispness of the air? And when the leaves have been blown away, do you not appreciate the shapes of the tree-bodies, the wider sky, the rolling snow-scapes and the immense quietude of winter?*

*Let the natural world show you that when forms fall away and the displays of plenty transform or are invisible, it is because energy and nutrients are being gathered for new life. You too can use times of change and seeming lack to prepare, restore and reinvigorate yourself for the next cycle of blossoming. If you enjoy and partake of each season of your life as an opportunity to receive new gifts and prepare for what is on its way to you, then you will experience even seeming lack as the call of plenty to compel new creation!*

*The vibrational attraction force in humans is feeling. Thus,* ***the key to having is feeling as if you already have****. So let's examine lack's more welcomed partner, plenty! What does feeling* *as if you already have feel like? Your most helpful feeling-allies for creating an inner and outer atmosphere of plenty are* ***gratitude, joy*** *and* ***optimism*** *– with these being fed by a* ***love of life*** *and a* ***sense of purpose****. When you love life, you say yes to life, whatever happens – because in life it all happens! And for the times when you have plenty of tangible plenty, remember that plenty too will have its seeming ebbs so that space can be made for new kinds of plenty to show up in your life in their natural time.*

*So, dear one, when you call upon the angle of Divine Light that my energies represent as POYEL, I will help your heart to say yes to life so that you may feel and be grateful for the support and plenty that already and always attends you from the inner and the outer – including that which is on its way to you from eternity into time. And as you forget your worries and concerns for more and more moments here and there to just be and love, laugh and live, we will surprise you with sudden awarenesses that we are the ground and the roots, the winds and the wings, the eternal light and inner realms that support you unfailingly, in collaboration and respectfulness for your own soul choices. For surely, like the 'sparrows,' you are always being provided for. Amen...*

# May 17 – May 25

---

## Angels 57 – 64

---

*Sephira 8*

## HOD ~ Splendor

*Overlighting Archangel*

**RAPHAEL ~ 'Healer-God'**
(Governs with MIKHAEL) Healing, wholeness, alchemy/transformation, harmony, awareness.

---

## 57 NEMAMIAH
## 58 YEIALEL
## 59 HARAHEL
## 60 MITZRAEL
## 61 UMABEL
## 62 IAH-HEL
## 63 ANAUEL
## 64 MEHIEL

* Note that the Archangel correspondences in Sephirot 6 and 8 have been interchanged throughout the centuries by different Kabbalists and schools of thought. After additional research which shows the ways in which both Archangels are active in both Sephirot, the primary Archangel correspondences presented in the original *Birth Angels* book are reversed here, but each are included as co-governing.

## **5/17** * 8/1 * 10/14 * 12/25 * 3/5

# 57 NEMAMIAH

(neh-MA-mee-YAH)

***Discernment*** (R)

*'One who sees through the eyes of the heart'*

Archangel ~ RAPHAEL (with MIKHAEL)

Capricorn / Uranus (1/1-5)

---

I AM THAT WHICH...

*helps you to see with the eyes of your heart in order to perceive underlying dynamics and give you a broader understanding of beings, behaviors and circumstances. Nothing in life is ever just black-and-white. Everything and everyone is affected by a rainbow of influences which can facilitate or impede the flow of life-affirming energies. Discernment is judgment with the wisdom and deeper-seeing of heart, and it mirrors the all-inclusive loving way in which the Divine sees you and all beings. Whereas judgment without heart may see only what a thing or being is not in the limited contexts of time and place; what discernment sees is totality, noting that some of that totality exists here and now, and some may still be in eternal time as potential. In effect, discernment is able to see even what's not quite here yet.*

*Examples might be the difference between what you intend to say and how it actually comes across, or what you plan to do and what has yet to be done, or who you know yourself to be 'on the inside' and how others perceive you outwardly. When you use discernment to make decisions or form opinions, you are acknowledging the flux of life. Thus you will weigh many factors both seen and unseen, known and unknown – even beyond any bias of your own knowledge or experience. You may arrive at the same decision or opinion in the end as someone making a cursory judgment, but discernment keeps all the factors and people in the flow of life, inviting possibility and growth; whereas judgment without discernment can foster impossibility and a repudiation of potential.*

*When Love is the life-affirming energy at the heart of all your decisions and relatings – then discernment works not only with the seeming deterrents of this reality, but also with the greater reality of Universal Oneness in which all things are possible in due time with the right conditions. Empowered by the omnipotence of Love, discernment sees the open window next to a closed door, the dawn in the darkest night, the anger that craves to be soothed, the hate that longs to be loved, the hurt that aches to be healed, the truth that wants to be revealed.*

*I, NEMAMIAH, am here to help you first see yourself with this loving discernment. For if you cast compassionate eyes upon the journey of your own becoming, the beautiful truth of you will become more and more able to show itself – and you will see the journeys of others likewise. And you will thus not be burdened by taking offense, harboring anger or resentment, or carrying around hardened beliefs and attitudes. You will be able to love and respect what is, while also welcoming what will be in the nature and time of its own becoming. I offer you my light to see yourself and all through the eyes of your heart, and you will see all in the light of possibility. Amen...*

**5/18** * 8/2 * 10/15 * 12/26 * 3/6

# 58 YEIALEL

(YAY-a-LEL)

***Mental Force*** (R)

*'One who lightens the heart to empower mind'*

Archangel ~ RAPHAEL (with MIKHAEL)

Capricorn / Saturn (1/6-10)

---

I AM THAT WHICH...

*helps you to harness the forces of Divine Mind in order to achieve the mental strength, stamina and determination to implement actions which can bring purity, truth, clarity and love into beneficial manifestation. We wish you to understand that any life-affirming force is not to be forced, but harnessed. The true nature of such force is not as an aggression or oppression, but an opportunity to align with the secrets of nature and the natural laws of the cosmos. For example, you cannot force a thing to grow or ripen without contaminating its quality. Or force a child to learn or understanding to dawn until a heart and mind are ready to open and receive. However, you can create an atmosphere of readiness that will allow you to utilize what a force offers when you draw upon it. To receive even a small portion of the force of Divine Mind, you must prepare your own mind AND heart so that there will be no distortions or impedances in the flow.*

*First, you must put aside any importance in what you think you already know so that you may have room for the new knowings that will come during your walk into the unknown. Secondly, you must open your heart and allow the sticks and stones held within to roll away, so that there will be no heaviness of feeling or hurt to weigh on your mind. Thirdly, you must allow your mind to be led by your heart, because only your heart will know what to do with the things that come into your mind. Only your heart will know how to guide and temper, take in and disperse the forces of Thought throughout all the parts of your being.*

*By these things you will be able to receive Divine Mind in a space of purity and without the need for self-aggrandizement. And at the same time, you will be willing to become the greaterness that Divine Thought charges you with in both receiving and giving of Thought to others. I, YEIALEL, am a light-bridge between you and Divine Mind. Know that to whom much is given, much is hoped for. But also know, even as the Mind of God knows, that everything you can know is nothing without Love. Amen...*

**5/19** + **20**am * 8/3 * 10/16 * 12/27am * 3/7

# 59 HARAHEL

(HA-ra-HEL)

***Intellectual Richness*** (R)

*'One who taps feeling and wisdom to enrich mind'*

Archangel ~ RAPHAEL (with MIKHAEL)

Capricorn / Jupiter (1/11-15)

---

## I AM THAT WHICH...

*helps to diversify and color your intellect with the intuitive and spiritual resources of your heart, as well as to remain open to explorations and perspectives from a variety of outer resources. A strong and discerning intellect is enriched by the higher knowing, deep feeling and far-seeing of the heart and its eternal resources. An intellect supported by heart loves the journey and is concerned not only with getting to the goal, but also with how it gets there and what truths can be discovered along the way that are enlivening and even different from its own.*

*Together, heart and mind each extend the capacities of the other. Drawing from heart, the mind has a greater ability to use its vast intelligence to tap many kinds of knowing, discern inner and outer patterns and make greater sense of it all. While mind can know and enlighten the world, only with heart can it change the world. Mind may know who you are, but heart helps you to become who you want to be. Mind can teach and rule, but heart knows that with love, beings can learn to teach and rule themselves. Mind sometimes likes to have the final say, but heart knows that for love there are no finalities. Heart shows mind the hidden things that need healing, mind helps to find the cure and then together they apply it. Heart gives mind a more depthful voice, not only making intellect rich and juicier – but more easily receivable, elegant, eloquent and transformative.*

*You have been given a two-lobed brain that is capable of holding both the art and science of life. You have so much more power than you are using, so much more knowing than you are letting in. I, HARAHEL, and all your Angelic attendants, remind you that by including your savory heart resources of feeling and wisdom, soul and Spirit, your intellect may amass more than the sum of its parts and become rich and juicy beyond your wildest imaginings! Amen...*

**5/20**pm + **21** * 8/4 * 10/17 * 12/27pm * 3/8

# 60 MITZRAEL

(MITS-ra-EL)

***Internal Reparation*** (R)

*'One who repairs what is torn'*

Archangel ~ RAPHAEL (with MIKHAEL)

Capricorn / Mars (1/16-20)

---

I AM THAT WHICH...

*helps you to realign with your eternal nature in order to heal the chaotic thoughts, emotions and actions that cause 'sins' against the Self, and perhaps others, which reflect a separation of consciousness between your inner and outer being. All outer transgressions proceed from some kind of ruptured harmony within, which is perhaps the hardest rift to perceive, endure and heal. The best scenario is that an offense to yourself or another is instantly apparent, and then you instantly work to set it right. The way it usually happens, however, is through an accumulation of more subtle offenses to self or others over time that foster a suppressed sense of guilt or shame and an underlying anxiety that can ultimately sink you into depression, illness, even debilitating forms of distraction or self-medication.*

*You are built to perform at your optimum when you are 'all of a piece.' Wholeness is when your inner and outer, Divine and Human parts are working together toward the joy and fulfillment of your soul purposes within your humanity. When you do something that goes against your true values/self/soul nature, even if the effect is not apparent at first, it is registered in the vibratory energies of your being, causing a vibratory disruption. If the situation persists, it will likely sooner or later broadcast into one or more parts of your being, especially areas in which you are most vulnerable. This is one of the ways in which physical illness or depression can seem to 'creep up' on you.*

*In your world it is common when you are seeking yourself to sometimes lose yourself on the way to finding yourself! Thus, you are given help from the light realms to continually course-correct, repair and be restored and refreshed. You are not alone here, for you are part of the great Oneness that resides within you and you within it. You are heard and felt, known and loved – before, now and evermore. Each time your heart heals, rifts are repaired not only in you but in the fabric of life. Each time you let yourself feel the Oneness, the veils of separation and forgetting are brushed aside. Each time you let love in, the stains of fear and forgetting are washed away. Each time you re-member your soul and its purposes, your body and mind begin to be healed.*

*I, MITZRAEL, am your inner light-doctor, ever at your service. Call out from your true and sweet inside, and I will quicken my healing energies within you to repair the rifts – and together we will weave your inner and outer back together. Amen...*

**5/22** * 8/5 * 10/18 * 12/28 * 3/9

# 61 UMABEL

(OO-ma-BEL)

***Affinity and Friendship*** (R)

*'One who thrums the threads of interconnectedness'*

Archangel ~ RAPHAEL (with MIKHAEL)

Aquarius / Sun (1/21-25)

---

## I AM THAT WHICH...

*helps you to realize that your humanity has a natural affinity with the Divine and all of Creation because your soul is a 'spark' of Divine Light, carried within your heart and from your heart to all the parts of your human beingness. It is your soul-spark that contains a light-print of the Divine Nature, giving your humanity an inner 'image and likeness' of the Divine being and its urges for creativity, individuation and otherness that play out within the greater context of Oneness. Over your lifetime, your soul-spark is an eternal flame kept alive by its Oneness-affinity with the Divine and by our Angelic presences as particular 'angles,' or qualities, of Divine Light within you which illuminate and amplify the qualities that will serve your unique soul purposes in this lifetime.*

*Such is our collective affinity that everything which exists in the heavens is brought to Earth through all you think, feel, do and become; and by these you are also known and felt in the heavens and all the universes. We who dwell within and among you hold the shimmering within your heart of this affinity between the inner (above) and outer (below), the Divine and the Human, thought and manifestation, feeling and fulfillment, God and you, you and each other and all beings on Earth, including the Earth itself. Together you compose, contain and dwell within the affinity of this great web of differentiated Oneness. And it is our great joy to accompany and experience each of you as you express your diverse qualities at different times and lifetimes during the processes and privileges of your human individuation.*

*Many of you feel or have felt during your time on Earth as 'a stranger in a strange land,' unbelonging and different from those around you. This is more natural than you realize, for many people keep busy so as not to feel this. The truth is that your deepest affinity is between your soul and the Divine Itself. But you also have an affinity to your life here because it is your soul choice to be here. So you are, by virtue of your dual nature as a Divine-Human being, a walker of two worlds.*

*Because your heart is a bridge between your Divine and human aspects, look to your affinities of feeling and intuition to know where your belonging is on Earth. And look also to your antipathies to understand who you are by who you are not. May all that you are drawn toward and away from help you to see that you and each are unique, beautiful and necessary hues of the great rainbow-light which illuminates the spectrum of the Divine within the beautiful diversity of your 'hue-man' beingness. There are no two beings composed of the same configurations of essence and form, qualities, potentials and purposes. Your differences are sacred because through them the diversity of the Divine Being is revealed and 'put into play.'*

*I, UMABEL, and all that is of the Divine (and there is nothing that is not), are here to help you to delight in your affinities of heart and mind shining from within and among you, even from within your outer differences. Amen...*

**5/23** * 8/6 * 10/19 * 12/29 * 3/10

# 62 IAH-HEL

(EE-a-HEL)

***Desire to Know*** (R)

*'One who calls you to the unknown'*

Archangel ~ RAPHAEL (with MIKHAEL)

Aquarius / Venus (1/26-30)

---

I AM THAT WHICH...

*amplifies in you a desire and passion for knowing – not only the things of your world, but those of the inner and 'other-worlds' as well. Your great desire to know is an imprint upon your soul, born of the Divine's desire to know Itself and what more can be made of It through your own human expressions, experiences, creations and relatings. As exampled by the enthusiasm of your earliest childhood, your innate desire for knowledge is what fuels the exploration and expansion of your world and your individual and collective lives. We, your Angelic 'soulmates,' are so utterly delighted to participate in your gathering of knowledge by amplifying within you the Source energies of Creation which you draw upon, knowingly or unknowingly, whenever you venture into the unknown to seek or know anything.*

*Know that all which is unknown is knowable. Your wise ones have told you that for any question you conceive, there is an answer waiting within you. And so it is that soul-knowing survives beyond the cycles of gathering and discarding of matter that forms your soul's physical vehicles. Whenever a curiosity or wonder comes to your mind or heart, we respond on our side of 'the veil of forgetting' to guide and help you remember what you already know on a soul level – and to support the remembering of your inner knowing with outer confirmations, coincidences, encounters, information and opportunities. Thus your knowing might be expanded into beneficial expression and creativity for the increase of your own true nature and the enrichment of your fellow beings and the soul of the world.*

*And so know this as well: I, IAH-HEL, and all the Angelic energies, are given to dwell within you because of the Divine desire to know how it feels to be in the great privilege and challenge of Earth-life through the unique way that you are, feel, think and do. So we thank you, dear one who is receiving this message in this moment, for allowing us to know these things through your unique beingness – and letting us feel your delight in every new moment of knowing that emerges within you and ripples throughout the chronicles of time and eternity. Amen...*

**5/24** * 8/7 * 10/20 * 12/30 * 3/11

# 63 ANAUEL

(a-NA-oo-EL)

***Perception of Unity*** (S)

*'One who sees the Oneness within the many'*

Archangel ~ RAPHAEL (with MIKHAEL)

Aquarius / Mercury (1/31-2/4)

---

I AM THAT WHICH...

*helps you to see the diversity of your own nature and of all things and beings as unique expressions of the inherent diverse nature and being of the Divine Oneness. It is a great paradox that you embody and are propelled by as a human being – the urge for individuation, which is supported by a seeming separateness between you and others – contrasted against an inner desire and longing for togetherness. This paradox that you live on Earth is an echo of the Divine Paradox from which you emerged as the many within the One, and the One within the many. Thus, you come to Earth to be separate on the outside, One on the inside. Separate so that you might have space for the blossoming of your individual potential and the flowering of love within the context of otherness, and One so that you may remember your soul desire to offer the fruits of your individuation to the whole in order to expand the Oneness.*

*It takes every single 'puzzle-piece' of you and all of Creation to make up the Bigger Picture of All That Is. Just as with the multitude of physical, emotional, mental and spiritual parts that make up the totality of your single being, every being and thing is a unique participant in the totality which composes the Divine Being. In the great 'uni-verse' poem scribed from the Name of God in endless configurations uttered across the cosmos, you are the dotted 'i's,' crossed 't's,' letters, syllables, words, metaphors and meanings of Divine Expression. Your differences are sacred, because each of you embody a spark of the Divine Light and Expression in a way that no one else does.*

*I, ANAUEL, am, and all the Angels are, differentiated 'angles' of the Divine Light, given unto you to illuminate and amplify the infinitely diverse qualities of the Divine shining within and through you. Use our light to see your own and each other's unique beauties as preciously as we do. For we know that your earthly eyes see 'through the glass darkly,' and the clouds of forgetting that veil the inner heavens cause you to lose sight of your true origin and soul nature. But there is a purpose for all that exists in the unfolding ways of becoming. You are not here to embody everything and everyone – only the love and truth of your unique self. As you magnify certain aspects of your particular soul within physicality, you thereby magnify and increase the whole of Oneness. Thus, we invite you to see and feel the Oneness-memory we keep lit within your heart, and to draw whatever you need of our eternity to fulfill your time on this Earth with all the love, beauty and purpose that you can joyfully give and receive. So be it, dear one, so be it. Amen...*

**5/25** * 8/8 * 10/21 * 12/31 * 3/12

# 64 MEHIEL

(MAY-hee-EL)

***Vivification (Invigorate & Enliven)*** (G)

*'One who brings the elixir of life to the vessel'*

Archangel ~ RAPHAEL (with MIKHAEL)

Aquarius / Moon (2/5-9)

---

I AM THAT WHICH...

*helps you to enliven and refresh your potential for an inner and outer 'greater life' by drawing on the Divine wholeness that continually brings you and your creations from seed to blossoming in each moment and season of your life to the next. As you siphon the energies of the eternal through your soul into your heart and your whole being, fatigue and depletion are met with replenishment and a fresh flow of nourishing energies. Your heart is the receiving vessel for the flow of creation energies that come from your inner Divine to be dispersed into your mind as new thoughts, ideas and inspirations that enliven and re-create your whole being.*

*In your lifetime, you play out again and again the cycles of creation, and your aliveness is felt throughout all of Life like a beautiful rippling of silk in the winds of time and eternity. You are as one strand in the web of life with the power to energize and enliven the whole web, and so the web supports and helps and heals and re-enlivens you in turn. Likewise in your life on Earth with other beings and with the Earth itself, it is vital for each to contribute to a nourishing atmosphere, supporting the growth and thriving of all. When you tap into the well of your heart to draw from your eternal resources, those resources are increased – not depleted – as they are released and multiplied within and among you. As it is with Love, the more you give away what is eternal, the more you have both in time and eternity.*

*So dear one, drink of our eternal light-elixir so that your thirst and ours might be quenched within you. Eat of our Angelic fruits so that our Divine seeds of life may find fruition in your beingness and in the world and the cosmos. Live so that the Eternal may experience its place and purpose in your time. Love so that your heart-cup of aliveness ever runneth over, forever bringing new life lovingly into being and doing. Amen...*

# May 26 – June 2

---

## Angels 65 – 72

---

*Sephira 9*

## YESOD ~ Foundation

*Overlighting Archangel*

**GABRIEL ~ 'God is my Strength'**

Guidance, vision, inspiration for faith
and connection to the Divine; vessel for
giving and receiving, creative fertility,
and the ebb and flow of life's seasons

---

**65 DAMABIAH**
**66 MANAKEL**
**67 EYAEL**
**68 HABUHIAH**
**69 ROCHEL**
**70 JABAMIAH**
**71 HAIYAEL**
**72 MUMIAH**

**5/26** * 8/9 * 10/22 * 1/1 * 3/13

# 65 DAMABIAH

(da-MA-bee-YAH)

***Fountain of Wisdom*** (R)

*'One who brings the ocean to the river'*

Archangel ~ GABRIEL

Aquarius / Uranus (2/10-14)

---

I AM THAT WHICH...

*helps you to realize the great paradox of life in which all seeming opposites are dual expressions of a whole which continually help to illuminate, facilitate and fulfill each other and reveal the greater Oneness of which each are part. Your heart is the bridge and meeting place between the inner and the outer, the Divine and the Human, your soul and your body. And your heart is your personal altar-cup that receives the flow of Spirit for your humanity to drink of in order to create meaning and purpose in your life and connect your individuation to the whole.*

*When you open your heart to your soul, your heart becomes a two-way portal 'between-the-worlds.' Here you may ask any question and the answer will be given, in one way or another, at just the right time. Here you may come into the presence of the great paradox of life that reconciles all seeming opposites. At this innermost altar is where the Divine meets and commingles with your humanity in a way that is utterly personal and yet distills and reveals your connection to the greater reality and totality of Oneness. Here in your heart, you may know all things, and be all.*

*It is my light-task as DAMABIAH to quicken the dormant seedlings of wisdom within you that knit together meaning and purpose from the piecemeal events, encounters and experiences of yourself and your world that preoccupy you daily. I am within you as the knowing that flows through feeling and knows by simply being. I am the* no - thingness *of your essence that is born from the All and knows that you are still in Its womb, even as you are looking to the seeming outside for everything that is already within. By my light is your wisdom born of our commingled flow of Love and Truth which reveals that 'the one you are looking for is the one looking.' Come and drink from the eternal light-font that I am so that you may remember who and why you are and see the beautiful wholeness of All within the whole beauty of you. Amen...*

**5/27** * 8/10 * 10/23 * 1/2 * 3/14

# 66 MANAKEL

(MA-na -KEL)

***Knowledge of Good and Evil*** (R)

*'One who lights a candle to cure the darkness'*

Archangel ~ GABRIEL

Aquarius / Saturn (2/15-19)

---

I AM THAT WHICH...

*helps to shine a bigger-picture light on 'good' and 'evil' as contrasting forces of expansion and contraction which propel the seasons and cycles of life and evolve all the diverse aspects and creations of Oneness in life and the cosmos.* ***Expansion****, or flow, brings forth creation, birth, growth, the waxing moon and the rebirthing light of Spring – and* **contraction***, as ebb, brings forth destruction, death, atrophy, the waning moon and the darkness and dormancy of Winter. Contraction, however, also creates a hidden momentum by withdrawing and compressing expansion until it can no longer be held back and the tide must inevitably turn toward 'shore' again. Just as in human childbirth, these contrasting movements helped to birth Creation and consciousness and continue to evolve and expand them through the ebb-and-flow cycles of life from birth to death and rebirth.*

*In the dense vibrations of Earth life the energies of both contraction and expansion can become distorted through fear, hurt, disappointment, anger, hate, shame, pain, greed and other extremes of emotion, behavior and experience. If these distortions accumulate for a prolonged time, they can cause imbalance, stagnation, inundation and ultimately the eruption of depleting and life-negating energies that bring harm to self and others and what you call 'acts of evil.' In your English language 'evil' spells 'live' backwards – and that, simply put, is what evil is – living with one's back to the light.*

*If you consider that all is God, and God is all, and there is no other, then consider this: when the Oneness of God began to differentiate and diversify into Creation, the inherent nature of the One became expressed through duality in order to create the means for otherness and relationship. Duality is a context for creation through both affinity and contrast between seemingly separate qualities and beings. Thus, masculine and feminine were no longer commingled in Oneness. Nor were light and dark, night and day, yesterday-today-tomorrow, yes and no, or good and evil, anymore hidden in the inherent diversity of Divine Oneness. Through Creation and otherness, duality and contrast of qualities, choices and behaviors were born – because in an Unmanifest Oneness God could not know the further potential that It was and might yet become. Having given the gift of free will to the life that comes out of Itself – just as you do with your own children – God empowered Its 'offspring' to follow your own paths of fulfillment, which thereby continues the expansion and fulfillment of both the Divine and the human parent.*

*Seen in this light, and considering that the density of physical life and matter pulls you away from the light of your origin, you can perhaps see how 'good' is an expression of going toward the light that is God-the Oneness and 'evil' is that which goes toward life and physicality, which is God-manifest as duality.*

*Much of the darkness around the concept of 'evil' comes from religious dogma and moralizing 'scare tactics' around some actual figure who can possess and influence beings to do 'bad' things. This is an outer projection of inner dissonance – projected outwardly in part because an outer other gives tangibility and relatedness that can help to define what you want to defeat. It is this same urge – for relatedness to 'other' – that also keeps God as other, separate from you and you from It. And this keeps you just disempowered enough to keep you searching for something outside of you to save you!*

*As the two-sided light of MANAKEL, I tell you that your true initiation and power as a Divine-Human being is to realize both the light and the shadow within you and to partake of their contrasting powers to continually move you from fragmentation toward wholeness. Allow the gifts of the dark to show you where healing is needed. Learn from the shadows the range and empowering contrasts within your humanity. Let your darker beauties give depth and texture to your lightness of being. Do not fear the dark or judge yourself because of it, for it comes to teach you how to love and forgive. Use the dark to recognize and bring forth the light, and the dark will be fulfilled in its purpose through you and in the world.*

*And finally, offer your willingness to love everything that comes from within you and around you, and nothing but love will have a hold on you. So may it be. Amen...*

## **5/28** * 8/11 * 10/24 * 1/3 * 3/15

# 67 EYAEL

(AY-ya -EL)

***Transformation to the Sublime*** (R)

*'One who illumines the inner star'*

Archangel ~ GABRIEL

Pisces / Jupiter (2/20-24)

---

I AM THAT WHICH...

*meets you in the depths to draw you into the higher resonances of your Spirit and Source. I am the soft inner light which helps to bring your eyes inward and lighten your breathing. I am the breath of love that whispers open your heart. I am the silence that quiets your thoughts and settles your mind...the full emptiness that allows you a respite from doing to simply be. I am that which draws you into the sea of wordlessness, where only essence flows and where you are buoyed by the light that always sees you, the love that never leaves you, the heart of the Divine that beats within you. I am the moving stillness of the eternal in which you may feel the shimmering soul of you and see your vital part in the whole. Rest in me...and slowly, may you see the pinpoint of light at your center, the inner star that is your eternal beingness, twinkling with your utmost possibilities in time and eternity. I am EYAEL, the sublime shining out from within you, through you, as you. Amen...*

**5/29** * 8/12 * 10/25 * 1/4 * 3/16

# 68 HABUHIAH

(ha-BU-hee-YAH)

***Healing*** (R)

*'One who loves hurt into healing'*

Archangel ~ GABRIEL

Pisces / Mars (2/25-29)

---

I AM THAT WHICH...

*helps you to return to harmony with Divine Love and natural law in order to create a balanced internal environment in which maladies and disease cannot flourish. True healing is about supporting well-being rather than fighting mal-being. Just as light without argument displaces the darkness, by increasing your conditions and potential for wholeness there will not be room for anything but light and well-being to exist within you.*

*Whatever your state of being in the meantime, however, in an atmosphere of Love all things can be used for the greater good. Illness can be your friend and informer, for it brings imbalance to your attention and is an indicator of where healing and 'correction' are both needed and possible. So let the Love inside and around you greet and surround any illness or malaise that has come to visit you. Honor it by listening to the message it brings to show you where and how well-being has been disturbed and what is needed for balance in your inner and outer life so that you may begin to heal.*

*As you move toward wholeness in attention, intention and practice, wholeness will be drawn toward you – for this is a foundational law of the cosmos: like attracts like, in that things, conditions and beings of similar resonance are naturally drawn to each other. Sense and feel the wholeness of Love that birthed you into life. See and taste the wholeness, savoring it in your imagination until it saturates your heart and mind with certainty. From here, the waters of wholeness will trickle into the tributaries of your entire body and being. Thus, come unto my light as HABUHIAH, and let us quicken the light-flow of life by jumping into the waters of healing together with winged heart-feet first, to love you into healing and well-being. Amen...*

**5/30** * 8/13 * 10/26 * 1/5 * 3/17

# 69 ROCHEL

(ro-SHEL)

***Restitution*** (R)

*'One who brings back your lost parts'*

Archangel ~ GABRIEL

Pisces / Sun (3/1-5)

---

I AM THAT WHICH...

*helps to restore the lost memory of your Divine origins and your joyful soul agreement to express a particular configuration of Divine qualities upon Earth through your own unique human beingness. In the wonderful and compelling aspects of Earth life, your attention is easily captured by the desires, demands, aspirations, challenges and difficulties, responsibilities and pleasures of life. However, because of the eternal soul-call of your inner nature, the offerings and preoccupations of the world do not completely satisfy you. There persists an underlying sense that something is missing or lost – hence the often indefinable longing for more, which can turn you inward toward matters of the spirit and creativity, or outward toward the acquisition of more and more matter, power or prestige.*

*I, ROCHEL, am here with and within you to remind you what you already know – that there is not enough matter or glory on earth to fill the yearning for 'heaven' in your heart and soul. Though at times you may get so used to living as a fragment of yourself that you mistake it for the whole, the heart of you knows better. True happiness is possible only when you live truly with all parts of yourself awake and engaged. My Angelic light within you is 'purposed' to help you do just that.*

*As you allow me as ROCHEL, along with all your Angelic lights within and around you, we shall amplify and give clarity to the muffled voices of your heart and soul. Together, we will put your inner and outer, Divine and human parts, back together so that you may become all-of-a-piece...with the peace of All inside you, expressing through you and as you for an awakened greaterness of your life on Earth. So be it, and so may you be. Amen...*

## **5/31** * 8/14 * 10/27 * 1/6 * 3/18

# 70 JABAMIAH

(ya-BA-mee-YAH)

***Alchemy (Transformation)*** (R)

*'One who turns base mettle into gold'*

Archangel ~ GABRIEL

Pisces / Venus (3/6-10)

---

I AM THAT WHICH...

*expresses the powers of the 'Great Alchemist,' the 'Transformer' of the Universe and Life Itself, to ennoble the base mettle of thought and physicality with a goldenness of wisdom and being. These are the powers that reach beyond form to change not only form itself, but the essence of a thing or person. For it is not enough to know the mysteries of life. For the fullness of life and love and truth, you must become them. The transformative light-force that I am in you is the same creation chemistry that turns a caterpillar into a butterfly, a seed into a field of flowers, an acorn into a tree and bare branches into a bursting forth of leaves, blossoms and edible fruit. From one cell into two, and trillions of cells into a human being, there is nothing that cannot be transformed within and about you for your greater good, well-being and fulfillment as a Divine-Human being.*

*All change is the impetus of Love to help you manifest more of the totality of who you are. When change seems to take some things away, think of those times as 'peeling the onion' – removing the outer protective layers to reveal the juiciest and most potent parts of you. You do not lose anything to change which truly belongs to you, only that which hides or deters who you truly are.*

*Your whole life is a dance between your inner and outer and a continual choosing of how much you will allow your soul and its mysteries to occupy your human substance and personality. When you invite our Divine energies to expand the Divine within your humanity, your vibrations heighten and your consciousness is infused with soul-light and Spirit. Your thoughts, feelings, being and doing, along with the base 'mettle' of your instincts, impulses, urges, desires and motives, becomes transformed into a life-affirming 'spiritual gold' which enables all your parts to be working together in the light of wisdom and wholeness.*

*You experience this kind of transformation in the deepmost well of your heart as the commingled grace of Love and Truth, and when it comes it is so profound and sweet that you cannot help but weep with gratitude and humility. It is a transformation which has nothing to do with knowledge or merit – it is about the willingness to open your heart to the Divine dwelling within you.*

*So I, JABAMIAH, ask you only: will you receive? Will you allow us and all that is Divine to co-create with your humanity to give you a most golden life? Amen...*

## **6/1** * 8/15 * 10/28 * 1/7 * 3/19

# 71 HAIYAEL

(HA-ee-ya-EL)

***Divine Warrior & Weaponry*** (R)

*'One who wins the battle that cannot be fought'*

Archangel ~ GABRIEL

Pisces / Mercury (3/11-15)

---

I AM THAT WHICH...

*provides a shield of Love and a sword of Truth to magnify compassion and clarity on the worldly-planes. The 'armies of Angels' do not fight the dark – rather we replace the absence or dimming of light with the wholeness of Light which has no seams or bounds. Darkness has its temporary stages and fields of play, but as in the beginning so it will be in every end – the dark cannot withstand this Light which all things and beings, including you, are composed of. Many in your world through the ages have known this and have worked to fill your dark times and places with light, knowing that to fight the dark would only expand it.*

*Others, however, have chosen the way of 'an eye for an eye' – but that is a shortsighted battle plan! When you love your enemy, hate loses its force, even if it may seem for a time to increase because hate, like all energies and emotions, wants to be expressed. But when love keeps coming, hate cannot feed itself and so must surrender to the light and be transformed. Remember this when you feel hurt or betrayed. It is not about martyrdom, but seeing all things and people through the all-seeing eyes of the heart. For love casts a transformative light on every action, enabling hurts to be healed rather than harbored.*

*This is what it means to be a heart-led and peace-full warrior of light. For the spiritual warrior's true battle is not a fight against evil, but a stand for good. The only victory worth winning is won in the heart, and thus must the heart of the warrior be willing as well as willful, malleable and yet strong, innocent and yet wise. Bring your Angelic heart unto the world, and the world will be changed. Thus say I, HAIYAEL: choose not the fight but the light. Amen...*

**6/2** * 8/16 * 10/29 * 1/8 * 3/20

# 72 MUMIAH

(MOO-mee-YAH)

***Endings and Rebirth*** (R)

*'One who uses endings to begin again'*

Archangel ~ GABRIEL

Pisces / Moon (3/16-20)

---

I AM THAT WHICH...

*helps you to look at endings in a different light, so that you may come to know them simply as vehicles for the continual evolving of your soul's expression in, or out of, the physicality of time and place. Ending times are your opportunity to let go of what is no longer needed in order to have the inner and outer room to create and receive the new. Throughout the seasons and cycles of your life, you are sowing, nurturing, blossoming, coming to fruition, harvesting, seeding, gestating and rebirthing. As much as you may want relationships and circumstances in your life to stay the same, things and people must flow and change because in order to thrive, life must move and evolve from what came before to the new that wants to come into being.*

*All of life begins and ends and begins again through the movements of contraction and expansion – like the in and out of your breath, or the birth contractions that bring forth new life. Contraction is a pulling in and back to gather a building force for the release and expansion of new energy and beingness. Likewise, endings are moments of contraction to clear energies and build momentum for expansion into a new beginning. We know that it is natural for your heart to feel sorrow when something or someone has seemingly ended. But we wish to soften your sorrows with the assurance that the flow of life is designed for your inherent renewal and ongoingness in one form and way or another.*

*It may seem strange for us to tell you that your ending times are very exciting for us! But we so love to see the preparations for the new life that desires to grow within and around you. And I, MUMIAH, and all your Angel lights, wish for you to know that especially you are not alone in those ending times when you may feel the most forsaken. When your grief or disappointment about an ending begins to subside, even a little, you will feel us – for indeed, we are here with and within you now more than ever to remind you that you are felt, known and seen. And we will be here with you in the pause of stillness that you may need until you are ready for us to help bring forth the new bold, brave and beautiful you. And so it is, dear precious one. And so you are. Amen...*

---

# Sephira 10

---

## MALKUTH (SHEKINAH)

*Relates to the Kingdom of Creation*

*and the Realm of Saints and Ascended Souls*

---

*Overlighting Archangels*

### SANDALPHON and METATRON

These two Archangels, sometimes referred to as "spiritual brothers," are arguably said to be the only two Archangels who were once human and taken up to the heavens without having experienced human death: METATRON was Enoch, and SANDALPHON was Elijah. Metatron's unmanifested creation energies in KETHER are finally manifest in MALKUTH and the SHEKINAH (feminine aspect of the Divine) which gives birth to Earth. Thus here METATRON is the link between the Divine and all of humanity, while SANDALPHON is the overlighting Archangel of the Earth and planetary "caretaker" who grounds Divine Love within humanity and the natural world in order to cultivate higher consciousness on Earth.

---

In the Tree of Life symbology, Sephira 10 is a "bridge" realm leading from the Angelic Heavens to the realm of saints and ascended souls, and ultimately to Earth. Therefore, there are no Angels (except Archangels) correspondent to this last Sephira of the Tree. However, it is included here in order to complete the spiritual descent of the Heavenly Tree of Life unto Earth as it takes root and branches out into, within and among the hearts of all humanity.

*Amen...Amen...Amen*

# Appendix I

***Your Personal Birth Angels***

---

## ***The 72 Angels' Days of Incarnation Support***

Your Incarnation Angel expresses the Divine Being and Will in human physical existence, will and life purpose. Their dates of governing correspond to the five-day period around your birth and the qualities, challenges and expressions of your physical being and purpose. If your Incarnation Angel corresponds to the first or last day of the five-day spread, it is suggested to consider your resonance with the previous or next Angel.

| | |
|---|---|
| 3/21 - 25 | 1 VEHUIAH – Will & New Beginnings |
| 3/26 - 30 | 2 JELIEL – Love & Wisdom |
| 3/31 – 4/4 | 3 SITAEL – Construction of Worlds |
| 4/5 – 9 | 4 ELEMIAH – Divine Power |
| 4/10 – 14 | 5 MAHASIAH – Rectification |
| 4/15 – 20 | 6 LELAHEL – Light of Understanding |
| 4/21 – 25 | 7 ACHAIAH – Patience |
| 4/26 – 30 | 8 CAHETEL – Divine Blessings |
| 5/1 – 5 | 9 HAZIEL – Divine Mercy & Forgiveness |
| 5/6 – 10 | 10 ALADIAH – Divine Grace |
| 5/11 – 15 | 11 LAUVIAH – Victory |
| 5/16 – 20 | 12 HAHAIAH – Refuge, Shelter |
| 5/21 – 25 | 13 YEZALEL – Fidelity, Loyalty, Allegiance |
| 5/26 – 31 | 14 MEBAHEL – Truth, Liberty, Justice |
| 6/1 – 5 | 15 HARIEL – Purification |
| 6/6 – 10 | 16 HAKAMIAH – Loyalty |
| 6/11 – 15 | 17 LAVIAH – Revelation |
| 6/16 – 21 | 18 CALIEL – Justice |
| 6/22 – 26 | 19 LEUVIAH – Expansive Intelligence, Fruition |
| 6/27 – 7/1 | 20 PAHALIAH – Redemption |
| 7/2 – 6 | 21 NELCHAEL – Ardent Desire to Learn |
| 7/7 – 11 | 22 YEIAYEL – Fame, Renown |
| 7/12 – 16 | 23 MELAHEL – Healing Capacity |
| 7/17 – 22 | 24 HAHEUIAH – Protection |
| 7/23 – 27 | 25 NITH-HAIAH – Spiritual Wisdom & Magic |

| | |
|---|---|
| 7/28 – 8/1 | 26 HAAIAH – Political Science & Ambition |
| 8/2 – 6 | 27 YERATEL – Propagation of the Light |
| 8/7 – 12 | 28 SEHEIAH – Longevity |
| 8/13 – 17 | 29 REIYEL – Liberation |
| 8/18 – 22 | 30 OMAEL – Fertility, Multiplicity |
| 8/23 – 28 | 31 LECABEL – Intellectual Talent |
| 8/29 – 9/2 | 32 VASARIAH – Clemency & Equilibrium |
| 9/3 – 7 | 33 YEHUIAH – Subordination to Higher Order |
| 9/8 – 12 | 34 LEHAHIAH – Obedience |
| 9/13 – 17 | 35 CHAVAKIAH – Reconciliation |
| 9/18 – 23 | 36 MENADEL – Inner/Outer Work |
| 9/24 – 28 | 37 ANIEL – Breaking the Circle |
| 9/29 – 10/3 | 38 HAAMIAH – Ritual & Ceremony |
| 10/4 – 8 | 39 REHAEL – Filial Submission |
| 10/9 – 13 | 40 YEIAZEL – Divine Consolation & Comfort |
| 10/14 – 18 | 41 HAHAHEL – Mission |
| 10/19 – 23 | 42 MIKAEL – Political Authority & Order |
| 10/24 – 28 | 43 VEULIAH – Prosperity |
| 10/29 – 11/2 | 44 YELAHIAH – Karmic Warrior |
| 11/3 – 7 | 45 SEALIAH – Motivation & Willfulness |
| 11/8 – 12 | 46 ARIEL – Perceiver & Revealer |
| 11/13 – 17 | 47 ASALIAH – Contemplation |
| 11/18 – 22 | 48 MIHAEL – Fertility & Fruitfulness |
| 11/23 – 27 | 49 VEHUEL – Elevation & Grandeur |
| 11/28 – 12/2 | 50 DANIEL – Eloquence |
| 12/3 – 7 | 51 HAHASIAH – Universal Medicine |
| 12/8 – 12 | 52 IMAMIAH – Expiation of Errors |
| 12/13 – 16 | 53 NANAEL – Spiritual Communication |
| 12/17 – 21 | 54 NITHAEL – Rejuvenation & Eternal Youth |
| 12/22 – 26 | 55 MEBAHIAH – Intellectual Lucidity |
| 12/27 – 1/31 | 56 POYEL – Fortune & Support |
| 1/1 – 5 | 57 NEMAMIAH – Discernment |
| 1/6 – 10 | 58 YEIALEL – Mental Force |
| 1/11 – 15 | 59 HARAHEL – Intellectual Richness |
| 1/16 – 20 | 60 MITZRAEL – Internal Reparation |
| 1/21 – 25 | 61 UMABEL – Affinity & Friendship |
| 1/26 – 30 | 62 IAH-HEL – Desire to Know |
| 1/31 – 2/4 | 63 ANAUEL – Perception of Unity |

| | |
|---|---|
| 2/5 – 9 | 64 MEHIEL – Vivification (Invigorate/Enliven) |
| 2/10 – 14 | 65 DAMABIAH – Fountain of Wisdom |
| 2/15 – 19 | 66 MANAKEL – Knowledge of Good & Evil |
| 2/20 – 24 | 67 EYAEL – Transformation to Sublime |
| 2/25 – 29 | 68 HABUHIAH – Healing |
| 3/1 – 5 | 69 ROCHEL – Restitution |
| 3/6 – 10 | 70 JABAMIAH – Alchemy (Transformation) |
| 3/11 – 15 | 71 HAIYAEL – Divine Warrior & Weaponry |
| 3/16 – 20 | 72 MUMIAH – Endings & Rebirth |

## ***The 72 Angels' Times of Intellect Support***

The following shows all 72 Angels in their one 20-minute period in the 24-hour day when they are governing the intellect plane, and thus expressing particular qualities of Divine Mind in your human intellect to help you cultivate awareness and higher-mind. Your Intellect Angel is the one that was governing 20 minutes within your time of birth at your place of birth. Thus, if you were born at 12:10 a.m., your Intellect Angel would be 1 VEHUIAH. Those born at a cusp time – on the hour or 20 minutes before or after – have two Intellect Angels; so if you were born at 12:20 a.m., your two Intellect Angels would be 1 VEHUIAH and 2 JELIEL – or you may want to work with the one with which you feel the most resonance. Likewise if your time of birth is very close to a cusp time.

Note that there is another system of determining your Intellect Angel that was developed by 20th century Kabbalist, Kabaleb (see Appendix II), from his orientation as an esoteric astrologer in corresponding the 72 Angels to 360 degrees of the Zodiac. With his system you must find out when the sun rose at the exact day, year and place you were born, correspond that to the exact degree of the Zodiac on that date, and then do a complex counting computation, which I do not have the resources for. However, Kabaleb's son, Tristan Llop (nuevavibracion.com) is happy to help you with that.

Also note that for those who use a 24-hour clock, 12:00 a.m. midnight to 12:00 p.m. noon would be 00:00-12:00, and 12:00 p.m. noon to 12 midnight is 12:00-24:00.

**12 Midnight (a.m.) to 12 Noon (p.m.) (00:00 – 12:00)**

| | |
|---|---|
| 12:00 – 12:20 | 1 VEHUIAH – Will & New Beginnings |
| 12:20 – 12:40 | 2 JELIEL – Love & Wisdom |
| 12:40 – 1:00 | 3 SITAEL – Construction of Worlds |
| 1:00 – 1:20 | 4 ELEMIAH – Divine Power |
| 1:20 – 1:40 | 5 MAHASIAH – Rectification |
| 1:40 – 2:00 | 6 LELAHEL – Light of Understanding |
| 2:00 – 2:20 | 7 ACHAIAH – Patience |
| 2:20 – 2:40 | 8 CAHETEL – Divine Blessings |
| 2:40 – 3:00 | 9 HAZIEL – Divine Mercy & Forgiveness |
| 3:00 – 3:20 | 10 ALADIAH – Divine Grace |
| 3:20 – 3:40 | 11 LAUVIAH – Victory |
| 3:40 – 4:00 | 12 HAHAIAH – Refuge, Shelter |
| 4:00 – 4:20 | 13 YEZALEL – Fidelity, Loyalty, Allegiance |
| 4:20 – 4:40 | 14 MEBAHEL – Truth, Liberty, Justice |
| 4:40 – 5:00 | 15 HARIEL – Purification |
| 5:00 – 5:20 | 16 HAKAMIAH – Loyalty |
| 5:20 – 5:40 | 17 LAVIAH – Revelation |
| 5:40 – 6:00 | 18 CALIEL – Justice |
| 6:00 – 6:20 | 19 LEUVIAH – Expansive Intelligence, Fruition |
| 6:20 – 6:40 | 20 PAHALIAH – Redemption |
| 6:40 – 7:00 | 21 NELCHAEL – Ardent Desire to Learn |
| 7:00 – 7:20 | 22 YEIAYEL – Fame, Renown |
| 7:20 – 7:40 | 23 MELAHEL – Healing Capacity |
| 7:40 – 8:00 | 24 HAHEUIAH – Protection |
| 8:00 – 8:20 | 25 NITH-HAIAH – Spiritual Wisdom & Magic |
| 8:20 – 8:40 | 26 HAAIAH – Political Science & Ambition |
| 8:40 – 9:00 | 27 YERATEL – Propagation of the Light |
| 9:00 – 9:20 | 28 SEHEIAH – Longevity |
| 9:20 – 9:40 | 29 REIYEL – Liberation |
| 9:40 – 10:00 | 30 OMAEL – Fertility, Multiplicity |
| 10:00 – 10:20 | 31 LECABEL – Intellectual Talent |
| 10:20 – 10:40 | 32 VASARIAH – Clemency & Equilibrium |
| 10:40 – 11:00 | 33 YEHUIAH – Subordination to Higher Order |
| 11:00 – 11:20 | 34 LEHAHIAH – Obedience |
| 11:20 – 11:40 | 35 CHAVAKIAH – Reconciliation |
| 11:40 – 12:00 | 36 MENADEL – Inner/Outer Work |

**12:00 Noon (p.m.) to 12 Midnight (a.m.) (12:00 – 24:00)**

| | |
|---|---|
| 12:00 – 12:20 | 37 ANIEL – Breaking the Circle |
| 12:20 – 12:40 | 38 HAAMIAH – Ritual & Ceremony |
| 12:40 – 1:00 | 39 REHAEL – Filial Submission |
| 1:00 – 1:20 | 40 YEIAZEL – Divine Consolation & Comfort |
| 1:20 – 1:40 | 41 HAHAHEL – Mission |
| 1:40 – 2:00 | 42 MIKAEL – Political Authority & Order |
| 2:00 – 2:20 | 43 VEULIAH – Prosperity |
| 2:20 – 2:40 | 44 YELAHIAH – Karmic Warrior |
| 2:40 – 3:00 | 45 SEALIAH – Motivation & Willfulness |
| 3:00 – 3:20 | 46 ARIEL – Perceiver & Revealer |
| 3:20 – 3:40 | 47 ASALIAH – Contemplation |
| 3:40 – 4:00 | 48 MIHAEL – Fertility & Fruitfulness |
| 4:00 – 4:20 | 49 VEHUEL – Elevation & Grandeur |
| 4:20 – 4:40 | 50 DANIEL – Eloquence |
| 4:40 – 5:00 | 51 HAHASIAH – Universal Medicine |
| 5:00 – 5:20 | 52 IMAMIAH – Expiation of Errors |
| 5:20 – 5:40 | 53 NANAEL – Spiritual Communication |
| 5:40 – 6:00 | 54 NITHAEL – Rejuvenation & Eternal Youth |
| 6:00 – 6:20 | 55 MEBAHIAH – Intellectual Lucidity |
| 6:20 – 6:40 | 56 POYEL – Fortune & Support |
| 6:40 – 7:00 | 57 NEMAMIAH – Discernment |
| 7:00 – 7:20 | 58 YEIALEL – Mental Force |
| 7:20 – 7:40 | 59 HARAHEL – Intellectual Richness |
| 7:40 – 8:00 | 60 MITZRAEL – Internal Reparation |
| 8:00 – 8:20 | 61 UMABEL – Affinity & Friendship |
| 8:20 – 8:40 | 62 IAH- HEL – Desire to Know |
| 8:40 – 9:00 | 63 ANAUEL – Perception of Unity |
| 9:00 – 9:20 | 64 MEHIEL – Vivification (Invigorate/Enliven) |
| 9:20 – 9:40 | 65 DAMABIAH – Fountain of Wisdom |
| 9:40 – 10:00 | 66 MANAKEL – Knowledge of Good & Evil |
| 10:00 – 10:20 | 67 EYAEL – Transformation to Sublime |
| 10:20 – 10:40 | 68 HABUHIAH – Healing |
| 10:40 – 11:00 | 69 ROCHEL – Restitution |
| 11:00 – 11:20 | 70 JABAMIAH – Alchemy (Transformation) |
| 11:20 – 11:40 | 71 HAIYAEL – Divine Warrior & Weaponry |
| 11:40 – 12:00 | 72 MUMIAH – Endings & Rebirth |

# Appendix II

## *Historical Background of the 72 Angels Tradition*

The 72 Angels and Tree of Life tradition introduced in my first *Birth Angels* book in 2004 has strong connections to the 12$^{th}$ century work of Rabbi Yitzhak Ha-Ivver (Isaac the Blind) in Provence, France (c. 1160–1235), which was reportedly carried forward and further developed by Rabbi Moses ben Nahman (Nachmanides, or RaMBaN) (1194-1270) and other Rabbis and scholars into 13$^{th}$-15$^{th}$ century Gerona, Spain. Although these men were working within the **Judaic Kabbalah**, there were notable influences and contributions from other mystical traditions, which give philosophical input to the Angelic aspects of the tradition: **Christian Gnosticism** (direct knowing of God through personal communion), **Sufism** (coming closer to the "inner Beloved" while still in life through love and unity-identification), **Hinduism** (the many "gods" as the many aspects of the "One Supreme Being" dwelling within and awaiting our recognition), **Neoplatonism** (espousing the "One" and the "Infinite" beyond being, from which all Life is brought forth containing the essence of the Divine One) and **Hermetics** (the Egyptian and Greek spiritual alchemy of transforming base *mettle* into the gold of wisdom and ennobled beingness in order to manifest Heaven on Earth). The spiritual pioneers of the Middle Ages and Renaissance who hailed from different paths believed in the right of all humankind – both men and women of all creeds and cultures – to have direct communion with the Divine without the dictates, prohibitions or exclusivities of dogma. This became an increasingly heretical notion as Europe approached the wide and terrible reach of the Spanish Inquisition that began in 1478.

**The Spanish connection from medieval to modern times.** In the 13th century, Nachmanides founded a yeshiva for Judaic and Kabbalah studies in Gerona (also "Girona"), Spain. He was a disciple of Kabbalist Rabbi Azriel of Girona, who himself was a disciple of Rabbi Isaac the Blind. Nachmanides was renowned for chronicling much of the oral tradition of the Kabbalah, as well as defending the Jewish position on Messianic doctrine in the court of King James I of Aragon in the famous Barcelona Dispute of 1263. He was subsequently forced into exile and passed the rest of his life in Israel. In 1492 the school and Jewish grotto were walled up and abandoned during the Conversion/Expulsion Edict of the Spanish Inquisition in which Jews were forced to convert to Christianity or flee. Many of those working with the Kabbalah fled to Safed, Israel, which yielded the works and influence in the 16th century of Rabbis Moshe Cordovero and Isaac Luria (the "ARI"), who worked extensively on the details of the Tree of Life symbology and are considered to be the fathers of modern Kabbalist thought. Today there is still a thriving arts and Kabbalah community in Safed.

In the meantime, the Gerona grotto (the "Call" or "Cahal") remained hidden for almost five centuries until a gentrification trend in the 1970's and 80's spurred interest in acquiring and renovating medieval properties. According to accounts given by Gerona historian, Assumpcio Hosta, to Dartmouth professors and travel writers, Myrna Katz Frommer and Harvey Frommer, restauranteur Joseph Tarres in the 1980's had acquired a number of properties in the grotto for the purpose of building a restaurant. During the excavations he found the remains of a medieval school which he subsequently learned had been the 13th century yeshiva founded by Nachmanides.

As recounted by Ms. Hostas, who ultimately became director of the Bonastruc ca Porta excavation project (to honor the Catalan name of Nachmanides), curiosity by the locals eventually turned into commitment as continued excavations revealed that there was once a thriving medieval Kabbalah community in Gerona that gave it a unique standing as the center of mystical Judaism in Spain. Medieval manuscripts which had remain untouched for centuries led to the discovery of hidden Hebrew parchments, and cooperations began with Yeshiva University in New York and the Museum of the Diaspora in Tel Aviv for research, cataloging and translation, which remain ongoing. www.travel-watch.com/spanish-jewish-con.htm and www.dartmouth.edu/~frommer/s_j_connection.htm

In the meantime, Kabaleb (Enrique Llop, 1927-1991), a Gerona native who was a journalist, author, Master Freemason, esoteric astrologer and founder of E.T.U, Escuela Transcendentalista Universal (School of Universal Transcendence), had already been deeply involved in working with the Kabbalah, referencing the lineage of Isaac the Blind, Nachmanides, Lazar Lenain (1793-1877) and others. Kabaleb also worked with renowned 20th century philosopher, teacher and esoteric astrologer, Omraam Mikhaël Aïvanhov (1900-1986), who lectured extensively on the mysteries of bringing the Kingdom of God to Earth within the individual through the mysteries of the Christ and aspects of Esoteric Christianity. Aïvanhov's recorded lectures by the Prosveta Society also include illuminations on the Tree of Life and the Divine mysteries, the Angels, astrology, alchemy, unity and more.

In addition to Aïvanhov's influence, Kabaleb especially referenced Lenain on the 72 Angels and their astrological correspondences, and developed it further into a more detailed Kabbalistic astrology which he outlined in his book *Les Anges* (Editions Bussiere 1989). As a boyhood friend and spiritual teacher of François Bernad-Termes (Haziel), some of Kabaleb's works on the 72 Angels were published in France under Haziel's name when Haziel moved to France from Gerona. Since Kabaleb's death in 1991, three of his four children carry on his legacy through their own work in the Kabbalah, astrology and esoteric healing modalities, as well as the publishing of Kabaleb's additional works: Soleika Llop, www.alchemiagenetica.com.es, Milena Llop, www.redmilenaria.com, and Tristan Llop, www.nuevavibracion.com). Thanks to my connection with Kabaleb's children through Linda Wheeler Bryant in Madrid, Spain, I am able to more accurately understand the contributions of Kabaleb in helping to revive and illuminate certain aspects of the 72 Angels tradition.

My own years of research of the Kabbalah tradition include certain works by Kabaleb and his influences, as well as multi-traditional sources spanning over 2500 years. I was initially introduced to the 72 Angels aspect of the tradition around 1996-97 by French Canadian and Swiss-French teachers Kaya and Christiane Muller, who now work with the 72 Angels and dream symbology (www.ucm.ca/en/info/the-72-angels). As my interest in the tradition grew because of its similarities to Christian mysticism, I continued with my own explorations, ultimately leading to the publication of *Birth Angels ~ Fulfilling Your Life Purpose with the 72 Angels of the Kabbalah* (2004 Andrews McMeel/Simon & Schuster).

A few years later I was contacted by Chairman Mike Booth of Aura-Soma® in the U.K. and learned that he and ASIACT (Art and Science International Academy of Colour Technologies) had developed their courses on the 72 Angels of the Kabbalah based on some of the material in my book. Finding similarities between the 72 Angels tradition and the philosophies developed by Aura-Soma founder Vicky Wall and her successor Mike Booth (including influences from Rudolph Steiner,

Goethe, Isaac Newton and others), Aura-Soma associated their consciousness-philosophies and colour-therapy products and with the 72 Angels tradition. During my subsequent 2+ years of working with Aura-Soma, I did extensive research, together with Dr. Sundar Robert Dreyfus, on the transliterated spellings of the Angels' names, which vary through the ages because of Jewish migrations and permutations of dialect from one culture to another. As a result, Aura-Soma now uses different spellings on some of the Angels' names than I use in my own work, which are derived mostly from the texts of Kabaleb and Lenain.

**Important Kabbalah texts and influences**. People are often surprised to learn that there is no one definitive Kabbalah holy book or text. The Kabbalah, which means "the receiving," was for centuries a mystical oral tradition that was developed within, but somewhat hidden from, Judaic doctrine and everyday practice. It is largely based on esoteric and oral revelations, studies of ancient wisdoms, inspired texts and inner receivings passed down through the ages from Rabbis, mystics and scholars to the next generation of disciples and students. The earliest known Kabbalah work, from either the 2nd century BCE or CE and arguably attributed to Abraham or Moses, is the ***Sefer Yetzirah*** ("Book of Creation"). This is a short but intense mystical treatise about how the utterances of the first "Creator Sounds," which ultimately became known as the Hebrew Alphabet, brought about Creation. It is the cosmology in this ancient work that Kabbalists through the ages have referred to in their understanding of the nature of the Divine and the act of Creation.

Another prominent work is the ***Sefer Ha-Bahir*** (Book of Illumination), first published in Provence, France in 1176 and arguably attributed to oral illuminations by Isaac the Blind. This is a collection of parables about a quote attributed to Rabbi Nehunya ben Ha-Kana, a Talmudic sage of the 1st century. A third work, the ***Zohar*** (Book of Splendor), is arguably attributed to Moses de Leon in the 13th century as possibly a compilation of the teachings of Rabbi Shimon bar Yochai from the 2nd century. This work has had strong influence on Judaic thought and doctrine.

During the Renaissance, a Christian Cabala emerged as some Christian scholars saw similarities between the mystical aspects of Christian theology and Jewish mysticism, but this has never gained traction in mainstream Christianity. A more popular Hermetic Qabalah was developed, however, which incorporated aspects from most of the esoteric influences of the time, including the hidden magical side of the Jewish Kabbalah, Western astrology, alchemy (from Greco-Egyptian influences), pagan (earth) religions, Neoplatonism, Gnosticism, Rosicrucianism, Freemasonry and more. Judaic and Hermetic Kabbalah/Qabalah became widely commingled in Renaissance thought, quintessentially in the work of Henry Cornelius Agrippa (1486-1535) with his *Three Books of Occult Philosophy.* In the 19th century, the Hermetic Order of the Golden Dawn developed the Hermetic Qabalah further within Masonic and Rosicrucian structures. Other influences were Francis Barrett's *The Magus* (1801), Eliphas Levi (1810-1875), Aleister Crowley with his "New Aeon" approach (*Liber 777*), Dion Fortune (*The Mystical Kabbalah*) and many more as the 19th century moved into the 20th.

In the latter "new age" of the 20th century, as the Kabbalah became popular among modern and new age seekers looking for alternate spiritual paths, many new Kabbalah works began to emerge illuminating various aspects of both the Judaic and Hermetic traditions. Some of these are scholarly works, presenting traditional views of the Tree of Life, the mystical meanings of the Hebrew Alphabet and more – and many others explore the tradition through symbolism, psychology, biology, Hermetics, "magick" and other aspects. One of my favorite works is *Simple Kabbalah*, by Kim Zetter, for its clear, lay-friendly and relatively short presentation of the important elements, aspects and history of the Judaic Kabbalah, including formative texts and certain Rabbis and Kabbalists who illuminated and preserved the tradition throughout time. However, except for certain works of the Kabbalah Centre and the Bergs, who hint at it from a different angle, "*The 72 Names of God*," and the works of Kabaleb in Spanish and French, along with Spanish and French translations of certain medieval and Renaissance works, the 72 Angels tradition has remained unknown to much of the world.

# About the Author

**TERAH COX** has worked with the Kabbalah, Christianity, Sufism and aspects of other spiritual paths and wisdoms throughout her life in search of the common threads of Love and Truth in their mystical hearts. In addition to the five-volume series of *Birth Angels Book of Days*, she is the author of *The Story of Love & Truth*, *Birth Angels ~ Fulfilling Your Life Purpose with the 72 Angels of the Kabbalah*, *You Can Write Song Lyrics*, and more. She is also a speaker, coach and mentor on the subjects of individuation and life purposing, creativity, spiritual development and the balance of individuation and unity. Drawing from the fruits of "extraordinary listening," she has used her writings, teaching and coaching as ways of discovering and sharing the Divine-Human mysteries at play within every being, circumstance and aspect of life.

Formerly a writer for the Aura-Soma Colour-Care-System® in the U.K., she was also signed to the music publishing companies of Columbia Pictures, BMG Music, Warner-Chappell and various European music publishers as a lyric writer of over 150 songs recorded for CDs, film and television. Her inspirational poetry-art designs for wall-art, greeting cards, prints and more are online and in galleries and retail shops across the U.S.

* * *

*Books & materials, speaking, coaching and workshops*
www.72BirthAngels.com | www.TerahCox.com

*Poetry art, greeting cards, prints & more*
www.HeavenandEarthWorks.com

*E-Cards with original music, messages and art*
www.MilestonesConnect.com

## BIRTH ANGELS BOOK OF DAYS

*Daily Wisdoms with the 72 Angels of the Tree of Life*

Volume 1: March 21 – June 2
*Relationship with the Divine*

Volume 2: June 3 – August 16
*Relationship with Self*

Volume 3: August 17 – October 29
*Relationship with Work and Purpose*

Volume 4: October 30 – January 8
*Relationship with Others*

Volume 5: January 9 – March 20
*Relationship with Community and the World*

---

Additional Offerings

*Birth Angels ~ Fulfilling Your Life Purpose with the 72 Angels of the Kabbalah*

Quick-Reference Charts & Posters:
*The Kabbalah Tree of Life*
*72 Angels of the Tree of Life ~ Days & Hours of Support*

"Daily Wisdoms" E-Mail Subscription

*72 Angels Day-Keeper* Journals

Speaking, Personal Coaching, Workshops

and more...

---

www.72BirthAngels.com | www.TerahCox.com

*You are invited to share your experiences in working with the 72 Angels by contacting the author at*
TerahCox@gmail.com

39813636R00141

Made in the USA
Charleston, SC
21 March 2015